IN TESTIMONY
Priestly Reflections on Medjugorje

Written by: Eighty-Four Priests

Edited and Published by:
The Riehle Foundation
P.O. Box 7
Milford, OH 45150

The Publisher recognizes and accepts that the final authority regarding the apparitions at Medjugorje rests with the Holy See of Rome, to whose judgment we willingly submit.

Further, this book is published with the understanding that the witnesses contained herein reflect the personal viewpoints of the authors involved, and are not meant to indicate the official position of the Catholic Church.

—The Publisher

Published by The Riehle Foundation

For additional copies write:

The Riehle Foundation
P.O. Box 7
Milford, Ohio 45150

Copyright 1992 The Riehle Foundation

Library of Congress Catalog No.: 92-064150

ISBN: 1-877678-21-X

This book is published as a "not for profit" venture of The Riehle Foundation. The established donation price of $3.00 per book is to cover its printing and handling costs and no individual, book dealer, or organization of any kind is authorized to establish a price for this book over and above the listed donation.

TABLE OF CONTENTS

DEDICATION

This book is dedicated to every priest who recognizes that special role of the Blessed Virgin Mary in the salvation of mankind. It is not important that they have been to Medjugorje—nor to Fatima or Lourdes. It is important that they have given their "fiat," first to Jesus and His Church, and secondly to Mary as their heavenly mother. They are indeed "seed of the woman."

ACKNOWLEDGMENT

A special thank you to all of the priests who have contributed their testimony herein. We ask every reader of this book to offer a special "prayer of thanks" in their behalf as well.

We also thank every priest who echos the sentiments in this book, but who were unable to offer their written statements.

The publisher acknowledges that the testimonies contained herein are the personal views of the authors and are not meant to represent the official position of the Church regarding Medjugorje.

Our special thanks as well to all the Marian Centers, Peace Centers, and Medjugorje Groups who contributed articles to us, or who allowed the use of their printed material to be contained herein.

May Our Lady provide a special blessing to the staff of The Riehle Foundation who arranged, compiled and edited this book, notably, Laurie Balbach-Taylor, Jayne Dillion and Bonnie Lewis.

The Riehle Foundation

INTRODUCTION

On April 8th and 9th, 1992, The Riehle Foundation received the following information from Sr. Isabel Bettwy of the MERCIFUL MOTHER ASSOCIATION. It originated via phone from Sr. Janja in the Medjugorje area. She stated:

> The situation in the country is deteriorating. Sarajevo has been badly hit, with the center of the city under heavy artillery attack. The airport there has been badly damaged. The attack went on all night. The Cathedral in Mostar has been hit. Evening Mass in Medjugorje was held in the basement of the old rectory, which has been sandbagged for protection. No one can enter or leave Mostar. Trenches have been dug and are occupied by the men of Medjugorje both on the north side of Apparition Hill as well as between it and Mt. Krizevac. They are ready.

Such has been the nature of reports and FAX transmissions we have been receiving daily for the past ten months regarding the greatest place of pilgrimage the world has seen in thirty years. As Sr. Janja has stated: "We know we are experiencing the Beast, as is spoken of in the Book of Revelation. But we are not afraid. We are in God's hands."

Has the prince of this world unleashed all his fury to eliminate the conversion process created by Medjugorje? It would seem so. However, this book is not being produced as an update on the events of Medjugorje or the evil currently in force attempting to eliminate it. Within these pages we wish to dwell on the fruits, as detailed by those who are especially qualified to discern them, the priests who have gone there, who have celebrated Mass there, who have heard Confessions there, who have returned to renew the spiritual lives of their own local faithful.

In the first ten years of the events of Medjugorje (June 1981 to June 1991), the fruits have been astounding. The response of the laity to the alledged call from Heaven has equalled that of Fatima. In fact, in 1990, the number of Holy Communions distributed in Medjugorje exceeded 1,373,800, slightly more than in Fatima (source Fr. Rene Laurentin). Literally hundreds of bishops have visited Medjugorje. It is not possible to keep track of all of them since, in obedience to the Church, they do not come in an official capacity, but as individual pilgrims. Some come "incognito" as part of their own investigation of this phenomona.

St. James Parish in Medjugorje has been able to keep a much more accurate record of the priests who have come, principally through their concelebrating of the Masses there. Through June of 1990, over 31,000 priests have visited the place of pilgrimage. With that said, let us get to the purpose of this particular book.

There are enough books on the subject of Medjugorje, and video cassettes to match. There has been enough spoken and written by both the proponents and the critics. However, there is a need to hear from some of the ordained who have ventured to Medjugorje in answer to the call: "Come and see." We wish to detail some of their responses in this book.

It is not possible to list all of them—or necessary. Seventy-five or one hundred out of 31,000 is but a small percentage. But, as the secular media has insisted for years, it is an accurate "random sampling" of what these special servants of Our Lord have experienced.

We have been privileged to speak with dozens of these priests who have made the trip. We even have been more privileged to have financially sponsored the journey for seventeen of them. Although their responses are predictably similar in most aspects, there is one particular grace that stands out among many, and that is the Sacrament of Reconciliation. So many priests who have gone to Medjugorje return to speak of the incredible Confessions that take place there. It is a phenomonon of Medjugorje, which has unquestionably become the reconciliation center of the world. It is the depth of the confessions that they speak of in glowing terms—true attempts of conversion.

As it should be, these spiritual healings are far more important than physical cures or signs in the sky. They also give the most credence to the discernment process of the priests involved. It certainly does not appear to be accidental that in this time of "forgotten confession and tolerance of sin," that Medjugorje provides exactly the opposite remedy in our search for God.

We applaud these priests who have taken the time to submit their thoughts on Medjugorje and the results of their journeys there.

We also recognize all those who have gone that are not identified in this book. Over one thousand priests from the United States have traveled those 9,000 torturous miles. May Our Lord and His Mother bless their efforts and response. It is not a matter of them chasing an apparition, or even whether or not they believe in it. Only the message being given there is important (it is an echo of the Gospel), only the fruits need be evaluated.

That is our intent here—to evaluate the fruits that these special "Sons of Mary" bring to us from Medjugorje. May Our Lord continue to strengthen their vocations in return for their response to her call.

The Riehle Foundation

MEDJUGORJE, A WONDROUS STORY

Fr. Bob Wells—Milwaukee, Wisconsin

Medjugorje means many things to many people. To some it is the place where the gift of God's peace was planted like a seed in humble and contrite hearts; to others it is a sign of contradiction and a testimony that is opposed; and for still others it is the hopeful cry of Heaven for earth's new beginning and the consoling presence of a Mother's love reaching out, near and far, to her dear children. While awaiting the final judgment of the Holy See in Rome regarding the authenticity of these events, one thing I can say for certain is that through the experience of Medjugorje, and by God's grace, I now know that I am one of Mary's dear children.

For any number of reasons, appreciation and acceptance of my spiritual Mother was missing in my life for many years. In fact, I had actually rejected and belittled her role in my life and in the Church. Today, for me, Medjugorje is a lasting sign of God's gracious call to conversion, a mysterious invitation to holiness and a prayerful journey into the Heart of Love. Allow me to offer you a brief portion of my sharing in this wondrous story of Medjugorje.

The desire for peace is what brought me to Yugoslavia in the first place. In the summer of 1983, while studying for the priesthood in Rome, I had the opportunity to attend a conference in Dubrovnik on non-violence and peace. During a weekend break in the conference, I set out on a skeptical journey to what was then an obscure village in the heart of Yugoslavia. I had little or no devotion to the Mother of God, but I went to Medjugorje to "see for myself" whether such a thing as an "apparition of the Queen of Peace" could be true. My first experience of Medjugorje initiated a process of conversion which has continued to this day. The beauty of the surrounding hills, the hospitality of the villagers and the prayers of believers opened a new horizon in my understanding of the phrase of Scripture that reminds us: *God's ways are not like our ways.*

After this first encounter in the village of the Queen of Peace, I would have to say that the dying to my own limited understanding of reality, both seen and unseen, was and still is a slow, painful process. The mysterious, hidden presence of God's Mother in my life began to draw me into a deeper relationship with her Son. I cannot prove it to you, but I firmly believe that Mary taught

1

me the meaning of her "yes" in my life: for me, this meant to have the courage to say "yes" to the vocation of the priesthood.

Mary's gift was poured out upon me during my second visit to Medjugorje on Pentecost weekend in 1985. Throughout the weekend, in my heart, I heard her calling me to "get into the midst of the people and allow their lives to call you to pray." Then on a glorious Pentecost morning, upon the "hill of apparitions," I experienced the love of my Mother bringing me new life and a deep inner peace through the power of the Holy Spirit. A year later, on Pentecost Sunday, I presided for the first time at a Mass of Thanksgiving, having been ordained the previous day.

In September of 1987 I returned to Medjugorje on a pilgrimage of thanksgiving. I went to thank Jesus and Mary for the gift of a year and a half of priestly service. This was the first time I was there as a priest and I will always remember the powerful experiences of God's grace touching and healing so many people in the Sacrament of Penance. Truly, the graces of conversion, forgiveness, reconciliation and peace are at the heart of Medjugorje. Flowing out of this third visit, I began to seek from God the graces needed to take up the way of holiness, to be a good confessor and preacher. My love for Jesus in the Mystery of the Eucharist and my desire to unite my prayers with Mary through the prayer of the Rosary continued to deepen.

However, returning home from Medjugorje was never easy and often I was put to the test. Painfully I learned through my weaknesses and failings that I needed to trust even more in the help of Jesus and Mary. Living the messages became a daily challenge. As time went on the desire to share the gift of Medjugorje with others resulted in my leading three different groups on pilgrimages over the course of the next three years. Each journey offered its own particular graces for the pilgrims and for me. Sharing the joy of our Mother and the peace of her Son on that "holy ground" is something we will always treasure.

My last trip to Medjugorje was in the summer of 1990 and since then I have continued to experience the intimacy of relationship with Jesus and Mary in my prayer and in my priestly ministry. The spiritual horizon of all that is seen and unseen continues to reveal the wonders of God in my life. I strongly believe that we are living in the Age of Mary and in the Time of Divine Mercy.

Clearly the presence and action of the Holy Spirit working through our Mother Mary in these latter days are bringing light in our darkness, hope in the midst of despair, and fulfillment of all that has been promised and is yet to come in the Advent of our God.

At the time of my writing these reflections, Medjugorje is under serious threat of attack from the hostile forces caught up in the continuing cycle of violence which has spread throughout this region of the world. My prayer is that the message of the Queen of Peace will at last prevail in the hearts of all her children. I truly believe that the power of the Gospel is greater than all the forces of darkness which oppress our world. Thus, as Our Lady reminded us in August, 1984: *For a Christian, there is only one attitude toward the future. It is hope of salvation. Your responsibility is to accept Divine peace, to live it, and to spread it, not through words, but through your life.*

Mary, Queen of Peace, pray for us.

* * *

REFLECTION

Fr. Charles Sellars, O.M.I.—New Orleans, LA

The invitation to pray is a rather common characteristic of the messages of Mary. Mary calls us to pray; she says she is with us; she desires to help us; she desires to guide us. We are her children and again she affirms us, she constantly reminds us of her love and protection.

Mary receives the Word in the purity of her heart. She conceived and gave birth to Our Savior and so nurtured the Church at its very beginning.

Mary accepted God's parting gift of love as she stood beneath the cross and so became the Mother of all those who were brought to life through the death of her only Son.

As we await the second coming of Jesus, we are in the presence of Mary. She blesses us with her motherly blessing and like our own real mother she adds: "Do not forget to live the message of peace." (From *Medjugorje Star*)

BEFORE AND AFTER

Fr. Tom Brunner—Cincinnati, Ohio

Pastor's Desk: August 6, 1989 *(Prior to trip)*

The week of August 16-23, I have the opportunity and the privilege of going on a tour of Medjugorje, Yugoslavia, where Our Blessed Mother has reportedly appeared regularly to some young people. Medjugorje is quickly becoming a popular tourist town due to claims of many miraculous happenings taking place over the last several years. I must admit that as recently as last year at this time, I was quite a skeptic about the whole phenomenon, but that skepticism has turned to curiosity, and the belief that there may be more happening there than I know.

Granted, there is a certain amount of hype associated with such a claim of appearances—things which many of us may not wish to support or be a part of—trinkets, tourist traps, etc. But deep down, something is happening there, I believe, something good. I have often said that I do not know exactly what it is, but that something good is taking place...lives are touched, faith is kindled, hope is re-awakened, love is in evidence. Anything which draws tens of thousands to join in prayer, and witness inner healing and conversion must have good in it.

Whatever is happening, I am grateful for the opportunity to experience it. I know that Mary has so much to teach us about how to respond to Jesus. I pray that whatever I find in Yugoslavia will enrich my own faith (and I suspect it will) and help me as I seek to enrich yours also! More in a couple of weeks.

My Report: *(Upon his return)*

In a way, Medjugorje was like coming home for me. I can remember in the third grade, when I won an essay contest on Our Lady of Fatima, and how knowledgeable and excited I was not so much about the contest, but about the phenomenon. Somewhere in the intervening years, the excitement waned. Do you know how I ended up in Medjugorje? It seemed a miracle in itself. There I was at Mass one day, talking about miracles and my belief that something miraculous was happening at Medjugorje, something that I didn't quite understand, but nevertheless, something...and at that Mass was a person who had that very morning demanded of Mary

4

that she indicate who should use an unused reservation for the pilgrimage to Medjugorje. Within three minutes of the final blessing, I had been invited, and agreed to the trip. And the rest, as they say, is history.

I could tell you about the fabulous trip, and describe my first experience of jumbo jets, European cuisine, and the Yugoslavian countryside, but you're probably not reading this for a travelogue...Besides, AAA could do a better job than I. What I want to describe in these few words is what happened inside me.

I did not see the sun spin, or my rosary change colors. Some say those things happened to them, and I have no reason to doubt them. What I did see were thousands of people from all over the world, speaking different languages, yet able to understand one another, because they communicated with kindness, gentleness, peaceful spirits, and warm smiles. When thousands of us ascended the Hill of Apparitions to support the young people who were that night to have an apparition of Mary, the Yugoslavian people led the Rosary in Croatian, their native language. We all responded, each in our own tongue. When I prayed "Holy Mary, Mother of God.." so did the people next to me, in Spanish, and French, and German, and Italian. And we all knew we were together, united by a stronger bond than a common language. I suspect the first Pentecost may have been like that. That sends shivers through me.

I did not see people throw away crutches and leap from their stretchers. But I did see people who came to Mass by the thousands, so many that in the evening, Mass had to be held outside, and I heard those people pray and sing like I have never heard before. In the morning, at the English-speaking Mass, there were close to fifty priests from around the world concelebrating, sharing their experiences of God in the U.S., Ireland, Africa, and a host of other countries.

I did not hear thunder in the skies. But I did hear the heartfelt confessions of people from around the world, who wanted to reach out and touch the God of their heart, and drink of His love, and know His forgiveness. Each day, throughout the day in the large courtyard, priests would "set up shop" and celebrate the sacrament of reconciliation with those who spoke their language. I heard the joyous talk of those who had come to find peace, and had found it. I heard people fifteen and people eighty talk and laugh and pray together, and join hands, and embrace one another at the sign of peace—perfect strangers before that moment.

I did not have any visions in the clouds. But I was able to dream of a world where weapons were no more, and where hearts were open to others. I was able to dream that because I heard the Word of God stronger than ever before. I was able to share my dreams with others who had traveled with me, adults, as well as many college age people whose level of faith and goodness assured me that we have a bright future ahead. I was able to sit one night with some of my fellow pilgrims at an outdoor pub, where beer and pizza rested on our table, and hear the people at that pub engage in a sing-along of Marian songs, and I thought, "isn't this wonderful?" That God and humans sat down at the same table, that strangers can enjoy food and drink together and at the same time enjoying singing of the God who gives joy to their hearts. That, my friends, is life.

Does a person have to go to Medjugorje, or Lourdes, or Fatima, or Guadalupe to experience all these things? Certainly not. But if I had stayed home, I don't know that I would have taken the time or made the effort at this time. When I came home, things were not much different than they were when I left, and the stresses and challenges were no less, but I have felt a renewed sense of hope for myself, for our parish, for our world. I feel a strength that I don't recall feeling before. In short, I believe that the phenomenon of Medjugorje is not a hoax. I believe that those faith-filled visionaries in Medjugorje really do experience Mary in a special way. I believe that all people who seek God, and want to touch God, and the people and things of God, will be able to do just that.

I am so very thankful for the opportunity to take a week of my life, and seek the love of God and His Mother in the simplicity of a little Yugoslavian village at the foot of a hill where stands a huge cross, a reminder of the power of love. My life will never be the same.

I COULDN'T KNEEL

Fr. Albert J.M. Shamon—Buffalo, New York

I have told this story only to a very few.

On a Wednesday, May 20, 1987, I made my first trip to Medjugorje. I was there for three days. I knew almost nothing of the apparitions there. A bit apprehensive, I decided to carry the Blessed Sacrament with me, as a priest would on a sick call. I felt if these apparitions were from the devil, the presence of Our Lord would raise a veritable hell with him.

At that time, the apparitions took place in the rectory across from St. James Church. The apparition room was a cleric's study. There was one door. To the left of it and half way up the wall, there was a bookcase. Above the center of the bookcase was a crucifix, to its right a sculpture of "Praying Hands," then a blank wall.

I arrived outside the rectory at about 5:30 p.m. There was a large crowd there. I was on the fringe. I felt I would never be able to get into the apparition room. Yet the Franciscan who guarded the stairway to the room spotted me. He beckoned me, parted the crowd and told me to go in. I attributed this to the Blessed Sacrament I was carrying.

The apparition room was small but crowded. I was pushed against the wall; but I was content just to be there. At about 6:00 p.m., young Jakov and Maria came with Fr. Slavko and knelt in the doorway and began to pray the rosary. They stopped at the third Sorrowful mystery. Fr. Slavko came into the room to clear a spot for the seers. That was just fine for me, because everyone in front of me was removed and I found myself right next to Maria.

The three of us were facing the wall, just to the right of the bookcase. The seers were praying the "Our Father" in Croatian. Halfway through it, their gaze became riveted on the bare wall. They fell to their knees as one, their faces transfixed on the wall; they continued speaking animatedly, but inaudibly.

Fr. Slavko snapped on the light so that those outside would know that Our Lady was present. It was a signal for all to kneel. All did—all except me! I tried to kneel, but my knees locked. I couldn't. So I bowed low in order not to attract attention. After the apparition, I left the room to concelebrate Mass, and my knees were all right.

The second night I returned to the rectory. Again, the custodian hailed me and told me to go into the apparition room. This was odd, for generally one could go in only once to give others a chance. I attributed this privilege to the Blessed Sacrament I was carrying. I went in; and once again when Our Lady appeared, I could not kneel. In fact, a priest tugged at my coat and told me to kneel. I told him I couldn't. I tried, but I could not. So I bowed low.

I returned a third night. I was invited in. When Our Lady appeared, I could not kneel. I asked Our Lady why. She seemed to say, *I do not want my Son kneeling to me.*

I left Medjugorje convinced of the authenticity of what was happening there.

* * *

Bishop Sylvester W. Treinen—Boise, Idaho

On the way to Rome, Bishop Thomas Connolly of Baker, and I, stopped to visit Medjugorje in Yugoslavia. Whether or not Mary is seen by the youths there, God is seen in the lives of all who live there and come as pilgrims. Conversion of lives to God is the wish of Mary for all of us. Conversions are visible in Medjugorje. I sat and knelt six feet away from Marija, one of the seers, though now 28 years old, a very normal looking and acting lady. It was an inspiring visit.

* * *

Bishop Donat Chiasson (Archbishop of Moncton, Canada)

A journalist: Bishop Chiasson, what is the reaction in your heart with respect to the phenomenon of Medjugorje?

Bishop Chiasson: What delights me here is that the whole parish tries to live the Gospel without compromise. I do not have an opinion to express on the apparitions in Medjugorje. However, I believe in the message because it is consistent with the Gospel. (From *Nine Years of Apparitions,* The Riehle Foundation)

* * *

Archbishop Patrick Flores—San Antonio, Texas

Archbishop Patrick Flores (San Antonio, Texas). accompanied by two auxiliary bishops, reported his dialogue with John Paul II in January 1989:

I said to him, "Your Holiness, numerous persons from my diocese go to Medjugorje. I did not permit nor forbid them. What should I do?"

The Pope answered me, "Let the people go there. They pray there."

Encouraged by this response, I said to him, "But they are inviting me to accompany them in the month of August."

The Pope answered, "Go, and pray for me."

It is thus that I find myself here in Medjugorje with the blessing of the Pope. (Remarks made in Medjugorje in August 1989, reported by *Message de paix,* Montreal, November-December 1989).

TESTIMONY OF FR. ABRAHAM

Father Abraham

I was born in Jerusalem of a Jewish family of 15 children, and I was raised according to the Jewish religion. Right from the start, a burning question haunted me: Who is the Messiah?

During the last world war, in a prison camp, I bought a Bible for the price of ten cigarettes. On meditating on the New Testament, I discovered that Jesus was truly this Messiah that I was waiting for. After the liberation, I was baptized and admitted to the major seminary of Monastere de la Dormition in Jerusalem. Then I studied theology in Italy, in Belgium and in Germany, and I became a Catholic priest. Do not call me a converted Jew, for I believed in God from the start, but after my illumination, I am no longer waiting for the Messiah. Like St. Paul, I am a Jew who no longer has a veil over his eyes, an "enlightened" Jew...

As I see what is happening in Medjugorje, I say to myself: The God of our fathers has had pity. He is about to shorten the time of our exile. Israel has returned. The "New Jerusalem" descends, straight, directly from Heaven.

Medjugorje is the greatest miracle in the world! Medjugorje is a second Israel. Mary, the Mother of God, comes there each day (since June of 1981) to speak to us of the essential. Since I heard about Medjugorje, I knew about it and believed it. Mary is the mother of all and the Queen of Peace. She comes to help her Son to save this world which is in terrible distress. To all the pilgrims of the Earth I would like to proclaim: Open your eyes and your ears...fall on your knees...and give thanks to God. (From *Ten Years,* The Riehle Foundation)

AN EARTHLY PEACE

Rev. John H. Hampsch, C.M.F.—Los Angeles, CA

In the months preceding the tragic hostilities in Yugoslavia, I had the privilege of chaplaining two large groups of pilgrims to Medjugorje (one of the tours being coupled with on-location production of videos for TV). My experience in that grace-enwreathed location left me with vivid memories that even today exert a powerful effect on my prayer life and ministry.

I regard these memories as forms of ongoing "grace nudges," some in the form of external phenomena, acknowledged as the most dramatic, though least important, of the events surrounding that revered locale. I recall such things as the enthrallment of the pilgrims I shepherded as they witnessed the daily "miracle of the sun," the various phenomena related to the cross on Mt. Krizevac and the many rosaries turning gold-colored.

But more significantly, I cherish memories of the extraordinary devotion of the laity, and especially of many priests with whom I had the privilege of concelebrating Mass (on one occasion, with 125 priests, 83 of whom were American).

Above all, I hold dear the memories of a sense of unearthly peace and serenity that pervaded the church of St. James and its immediate backdrop, especially at the time of the afternoon apparitions of Our Lady to the visionaries. The soul-hushing tranquility, which lended itself to such a spirit of prayer and sacrifice, had to do more with ambience than with externally observable events; and for that very reason, perhaps, it was more impressive than mere phenomena. In a very real way, Mary, as Queen of Peace, seemed to spread an aura of peace like manger straw, to prepare for the Prince of Peace to be inscribed in our hearts.

In that atmosphere it became clear to me that only when our hearts are all converted *interiorly* to be at peace *with* God, so as to experience the peace *of* God, can his true peace flourish *exteriorly* between persons, spouses, family members, religious denominations, ethnic groups, races, and ultimately nations. In this milieu, the true message of the gentle Queen of Peace of Medjugorje impacted my soul, wordlessly but overwhelmingly.

TESTIMONY REV. JOSEPH M. DOYLE, S.S.J.

New Orleans, Louisiana

Life begins at fifty! At least it did for me. A month after my fiftieth birthday I went to Medjugorje for the first time, to celebrate the feast of Christmas, 1988.

The trip from New York to Yugoslavia got off to a bad start in that we went, unscheduled, from New York to Chicago to Belgrade, arriving ten hours late and thus missing a whole day of experiences. Need I say anything about JAT airlines? Once we were settled in a freezing cold room, my good friend, Father Francis Butler, S.S.J., asked me, "Do you want to come back here next year?" "Never," I replied. "What do people see in this place?"

My question was answered on Christmas Eve on Apparition Hill. All bundled up, we joined Ivan and his prayer group in saying the Rosary and singing Christmas carols as we awaited the visit from "The Gospa." Many tears were shed that night by people whose private thoughts traveled so many miles and years in a way that can happen only on Christmas Eve.

In a moment of silence Mary appeared to Ivan. He said she was dressed in gold and was accompained by three angels. She asked those assembled to turn over their problems to her, and she said that the next few days would be special ones of blessings, graces and peace. She blessed everyone there.

I saw nothing, but sensed everything: the presence of the triune God and the thrice blessed Virgin Mary, the saints and holy angels, the departed members of my family, and such an overwhelming awareness of God's mercy and forgiveness of my many sins. Our Lady's message of peace took root deep down in my heart that night, and it has been there ever since. In the words of St. Elizabeth I began to ask myself, "Who am I that the Mother of my Lord should come to me?"

After descending the hill we went directly to St. James Church for Midnight Mass, which was attended mainly by local people. Pilgrims were thoughtful enough to let the people of Medjugorje find room in their own church on Christmas Eve.

When Father Butler and I returned to our cold room I said (with a very bad cold and all!) "I think I'm ready to come back here again." And so I did, in 1989 and 1990. My life, my priesthood has not been the same since. I am eternally grateful for the Divine Mercy of Jesus, for the motherly love of the Immaculate Heart of Mary, the Rosa Mystica, for the protection and companionship of the Holy Angels, and for the prayers of the Communion of Saints. I now have a greater appreciation of my priesthood and the Eucharist and a desire to pray and work for the sanctification of my brother priests. But I am also aware that I don't fast and pray from the heart as I should. My pride still gets the best of me and weaknesses of all kinds are a part of my life. Oh, to be fifty again!

* * *

"MATER ECCLESIA"

Fr. Stephen Josten, O.C.

For our times, I believe that Mary truly seems to be showing herself as a mother, "Mater Ecclesia," to the young people of St. James Parish, and through these young people she seems to be continuing her work at the foot of the Cross, co-operating in our redemption by her motherly concern and admonitions, as she did at Knock and Lourdes and Fatima in years gone by. Praised be Jesus Christ Who has given us such a loving Mother! I also believe these warnings, these messages of the Gospa are particularly urgent for the world of our time.

According to the visionaries, Our Lady has come here and continues to come with many messages for the world. As long as these messages are in conformity with her Son's Gospel, we want to take all of these messages to heart. We want to live the messages too, the messages of Peace and Reconciliation, the messages of daily Bible reading, of forming Prayer Groups, of daily praying the Rosary, of monthly Confessions, of love for the Mass. The time is short, "You know not the day or the hour," said Jesus. He further tells us: "I have chosen you from the world to go and bear fruit that will last." (From a homily in Medjugorje, 1988)

A BISHOP'S PERSPECTIVE ON MEDJUGORJE

Bishop Nicholas D'Antonio—New Orleans, Louisiana

It was not until 1986 that I first heard of Medjugorje. My reaction? "There goes Mom again!" I sought information and was rewarded with abundant material. The volume that powerfully convinced me was the excellent study by the Mariologist, the Rev. René Laurentin, titled: IS THE VIRGIN MARY APPEARING AT MEDJUGORJE? In fairness, I also read material rabidly against the apparitions, dubbing the Franciscans and the seers shameless frauds. With pain in my heart, I also read the latest document by Bishop Pavao Zanic who still does not believe. I very much enjoyed and admired Father René Laurentin's tactful courteous rebuttal.

It was in the latter part of August, 1986, that I was asked to accompany (not lead) a pilgrimage to Medjugorje. I refused. My reason: why go all that distance and expense to witness to something I already believed in? Then a kind person offered to pay my way. My Franciscan response was "you bet!" To get something for nothing, I could not refuse! (OFM).

At the outset, I strongly preface my Medjugorje journey with these words: **As Bishop, I do not and cannot speak to you officially. What I describe is only my personal and sincere opinion. I am under obedience to the Holy See.**

I was one pilgrim out of a group of priests, one nun and laity, organized by the Center for Peace, located in Concord, Massachusetts, U.S.A. The ocean crossing and the scenic bus ride from Dubrovnik to Medjugorje were for me strictly penitential. (Not a vacation!) All I wanted to do was go to bed! The bus was stopped only once by a policeman who scanned the group carefully and then surprised us by saying: "I am a Catholic. Pray for me."

We were warned to be most courteous with the Communist authority. The vehicle arrived just in time to attend the 7 p.m. Mass in the church of St. James in Medjugorje. The jet-lag dampened my fervor. I still wanted to go to bed. My companions, to my embarrassment, insisted they wanted to attend Mass. Ah, the good example of the laity!

Thursday, September 11, 1986. The church was filled to capacity. The sanctuary was packed with clergy, and I was the only bishop. It was stiflingly hot. The homily in Croatian seemed to go on forever. Even so, I was inspired by the deep reverence and devotion of the people.

Friday, September 12, 10:00 A.M. I concelebrated Mass for the English speaking. The main celebrant, an Englishman, rambled on in his homily from Genesis to Revelation, or so it seemed to us priests in the sanctuary. Then, to my surprise, a Jesuit priest, Richard Foley, (a renouned defender of Medjugorje), sitting next to me prevailed upon me to say a few words. In my heart I believed that more than enough had been said. I also felt it was risky to speak, being a bishop. On the way to the microphone, I spotted a large unconsecrated host on the credence table, took it in my hands and questioned the congregation: "Do you believe that this altar bread once consecrated by a duly authorized Catholic priest, becomes the very Body of Jesus?" The response was a loud "yes" I continued, "I guess that is the situation with the apparitions. The seers see and hear, but we don't. We simply believe them as you and I believe that Jesus is present in the Blessed Sacrament. It comes down to this: you either believe it or not. You take it from there!" (The applause surprised me!).

That evening at 5:30, the priests in our group were permitted to enter the room of the apparitions. Father Slavko Barbaric forbade the use of cameras. However, an exception was made for a BBC TV team. (Much later it produced a professional, well-balanced documentary on the events.) At approximately 5:30 p.m., Maria Pavlovic and Jacov Colo, were escorted into the study-bedroom of the rectory by Father Slavko. Outside, a priest was leading the Rosary and the response came in a harmonious jumble of languages. For me this was to be the great moment, an unmerited grace!

Maria and Jacov knelt on their heels inside the door to the study. They alternated praying the beads. Between decades Latin hymns were sung. The small room was so crowded hardly anyone could move. The seers, at a sign known only to them, suddenly arose and knelt before a sofa behind which was a bookcase and, on the wall, a crucifix and plastic praying-hands. I thought: "Surely Mary could have chosen a better place than this to appear to Her children!" I apologized mentally.

Maria and Jacov continued to pray audibly for a while longer. Suddenly both knelt bolt upright and fixed their gazes on a spot on the wall, wrapped in ecstasy. Everyone was kneeling but me! I just could not get to my knees, try as I might, so pressed in I was by those near me! I was embarrassed. I stared at the spot where Mary was appearing and apologized. In under two minutes the vision was over. The kids got to their feet and were escorted to the church for Holy Mass.

I was amazed at how serene the two appeared. For them, it was just another day! I myself was overwhelmed at the simplicity of it all. I reflected on how easily I believed in the Divine Presence. In that blessed room, I looked directly at the Mother of God, a reality I could not see with my eyes but which I accepted in faith to be true (just like the consecrated altar bread!) I felt so privileged, so blessed!

On the Feast of the Exultation of the Cross, several priests, laity, an elderly nun and I agreed to begin the climb to the top of the Hill of the Cross. Going up we prayed the Way of the Cross which gave us a chance to catch our breath. With us was a heavy-set female pilgrim whom we tried to dissuade from climbing the hill. She ignored our pleas and asked me to assist her by pushing her forward. So, with my left hand on her ample posterior, all of us finally made it to the summit. Once there, the good lady whom I assisted suddenly prostrated herself at the base of the huge cement cross and cried and prayed in the following fashion: "Thank You, Jesus! I praise You and I love You. You got me up here; I will be forever grateful!" I was miffed by her words and the thought came to me that, without me, she could never have made it!

The priests and I began to pray the Liturgy of the Hours. Our backs were against the rising sun. After a while I turned my head to look at the sun and got the surprise of my life! I saw huge concentric circles spin outward from the center of the fireball in all directions. In the face of the sun I could observe, as it were, revolving crystal balls of different colors—green, red, gold, purple! I motioned to the others to come look and see. We compared what we saw and agreed that we were witnessing the same phenomenon.

As the sun climbed higher, the heat became more intense, but bearable. Pilgrims from many nations were scrambling up the steep mountainside from all directions, singing and praying with great devotion and faith. The summit was already overcrowded, yet the pilgrims pressed forward and sat wherever they could. I was exhausted from sitting. I stood up for a brief moment and lost my piece of the rock. The new neighbor simply looked up and smiled.

At last the hour for the celebration of the Holy Sacrifice of the Mass arrived. The overworked pastor, Father Tomislav Pervan, presided. Even before beginning the Mass, the pastor entoned hymn after hymn and prayed for a long time. His homily was extremely long, and the intense heat made it seem never to end.

On the premises was the BBC TV crew, filming every detail, perched on top of a precarious wooden tower previously constructed for the occasion. The Mass over, we began the downhill trek. If going up the mountain was difficult, coming down was much more so. The loose rocks, the brambles, the pressing crowd, the cloud of dust and the smell of sweat was overwhelming. I, myself, was physically exhausted, so much so that my legs would tremble almost out of control at every step. Others of our group experienced the same. We stumbled, slipped often and were pricked by thorns, but no one was seriously injured. Later, word spread that a man had broken his ankle but was healed before returning to the states. When we reached the main road, we learned that the taxi drivers were given a day off to honor the Exultation of the Cross. Pure penance for us!

On Tuesday, September 16, the pastor, Father Tomislav Pervan, spoke to us in a cemetery about penance and fasting as Mary had instructed. What pleased me was how we ought to go about fasting on bread and water. We were not to starve ourselves. We should eat all the bread we need. Even so, bread and water make an awful combination! A good penance, however for those who can do it without harm to their health. Of course, Father Pervan explained, a person may fast in other ways.

On September 18, the buses drove the pilgrims to Dubrovnik for a day of rest. We were then homebound to the U.S.A., tired but spiritually affirmed and uplifted.

Allow me to describe what is happening in New Orleans. Due to the thousands of favorable testimonies given by the pilgrims (professionals, as well as ordinary folks), conversions are taking place. It is a kind of conversion which touches the deepest recesses of the heart and opens the eyes to the ugliness of sin and the need for peace, the fruit of a sincere confession.

Our Lady, Queen of Peace, through her chosen visionaries and her astoundingly simple messages, inspires the returning pilgrims and those who hear them, to implement what is asked of them. Prayers from the heart, frequent confession, fasting and Mass attendance become the basic means of sustaining the conversion process. With few exceptions, pilgrims become instant Marian missionaries for Jesus. Witnessing takes place in Catholic and Protestant churches, in hotel ballrooms and private homes. Two Channel 8 reporters, Jim Bailey and Mary Lou McCall, Protestant and Catholic respectively, accept invitations to speak anywhere concerning their conversion due to their visit to Medjugorje as objective reporters. Today, Mary Lou McCall co-anchors a religious news show called "Focus" with retired Archbishop Philip Hannan on Channel 32 WLAE at 8:30 p.m.

In parish churches open to the monthly Marian Peace Mass, the format is practically the same as that in the parish of St. James, namely, the praying of the Rosary while priests hear confession, followed by several testimonies, the celebration of the Holy Eucharist, and ending with the recitation of seven Our Fathers, seven Hail Marys, seven Glorys and the Apostle's Creed in honor of the Holy Cross. In some cases, a healing service follows.

I don't recall in history anything comparable to the Medjugorje event. How much longer will it continue? And what about the promised sign? It is anyone's guess. As a brother bishop, I have compassion for bishops who may have to confront the mystery of the supernatural as it unfolds in various ways, especially Marian, in their dioceses. It is no easy burden to shoulder! How true it is that God's ways are not mankind's ways.

What convinces me concerning this subject, is the profound faith of the people of God and the fact that the visionaries and the Franciscans have not gone mad under the pressure!

THE GOD OF RECONCILIATION

Fr. James Holup—Askum, Illinois

During the International Youth Festival in the summer of 1989, Medjugorje was crowded with young people. We were in front of St. James Church preparing in prayer for the evening apparitions. I spotted a young lad walking by with a "mohawk" haircut, earrings in each ear, and tatoos all over. My first impression was that it was a strange anomaly, and he certainly attracted everyone's attention. A punk rocker perhaps? A very strong spiritual message suddenly came to mind from the Lord: "This young man needs a prayer; pray for him." So I asked everyone around me to say a prayer for him.

Several days later, early in the afternoon, I decided to go to the Adoration Chapel to pray. Along the way I intended to help out hearing confessions, but no one was in the confession area except one priest with one penitent so I continued on. Then, this message came to me very strongly: "But I thought you said you were going to hear confessions!" I found myself answering the voice, feeling like I was talking to myself, and replied: 'But there's nobody here.' Again I heard the message: "You said you were going to hear confessions. Why don't you just do it?"

So I went back, sat down and placed the "English" sign on the ground next to me. Immediately a person from our group walked up, sat down and went to confession. I was surprised because I thought I had walked alone to the Church. As soon as that person got up, the same young man we had prayed for sat down beside me. I now knew why I had been urged to stay. When his confession was over, I felt called to give the boy my own copy of the book, "Pray With The Heart." I was suddenly aware of the power of that prayer that we had all said for him, and of the power of the Holy Spirit which called him to return to the sacraments. There were thousands of people and many priests in Medjugorje at that time, and yet in that one moment, I was there, and he was there.

(A rather dramatic actual photograph of the above confession made the cover of MEDJUGORJE MAGAZINE. A complete article by Fr. Holup on the event was included in that issue.)

IT CHANGED MY LIFE

Fr. R. Waguespack—Vacherie, LA

Medjugorje is a very important experience for me. It changed my life.

In June 1989, I came to the realization that Mary was really appearing to the children in Medjugorje. I also came to a crossroad in my life. I realized that I was not the priest that I felt I should be. Something was really lacking in my life. I felt that I had faith. I thought that I was always teaching truth. But something seemed to be missing.

So in June 1989, I determined that I really needed to go to Medjugorje to ask Mary's assistance in my life. I wanted to appreciate my priesthood more. I wanted to appreciate the Eucharist more. I wanted to be able to preach better. And I was concerned about my Parish. So I went to Medjugorje with these intentions in mind, already believing that Mary was truly appearing in Medjugorje.

What happened to me was nothing short of a tremendous grace. In Medjugorje my prayers began to be answered. I experienced a conversion, a surrendering to God.

Once I experienced this surrender, God began to pour out His blessings upon me, and I began to realize the workings of the Holy Spirit in my life.

Through the intercession of Mary in Medjugorje, she led me to her son Jesus, to a much greater appreciation of the Eucharist and of the priesthood, and has enabled me to proclaim the Word of God much better. This all happened through a quickening of the Holy Spirit in my life. I think it would be true to say: "to Jesus through Mary," and "to the Holy Spirit through Jesus."

So Mary led me to Jesus, and through the intercession of Jesus, especially His intercession on the cross, the Father poured out His Spirit upon me. I came to a realization of the workings of the Holy Spirit in my life. My life has not been the same since. Certainly I have experienced a much much greater joy. I learned through reading the messages of Medjugorje that the gift that we should really seek of Jesus is the gift of His Holy Spirit.

On my later trips to Medjugorje, especially my second trip, I put that request number one on my list; I prayed that God would pour out His Spirit upon me, and enable me to minister to people as He ministered to them, with the same love for people that He had. I feel through personal experience that this prayer was answered, and sometimes in a very powerful and humbling way.

I thank Mary for bringing me to Medjugorje. It is through her presence, her prayer and her intercession that I was led to an appreciation of the gifts that God has given to me. I am going back as soon as I can. I continue to go back to Medjugorje because every trip to Medjugorje builds on the first. I was not able to absorb everything that God had in store for me with one visit.

I hope and pray others will have the same type of experience of Mary, of Jesus, and of the Holy Spirit. (From *The Medjugorje Star*)

* * *

GET BACK TO THE BASICS

Fr. Michael Goergen—Chicago, Illinois

My trip to Medjugorje was a very memorable one because it revived for me my devotion to Our Blessed Lady. I went with my mother who has a very strong and meaningful devotion to Our Lady.

I am deeply convinced that the Lord has touched Medjugorje by allowing the visions to take place. The message is simple: "Get back to basics." Turn to God and love Him, and each other. Isn't this what we've been preaching for years? Our Lady is reminding us of this basic important stance in our lives. I am grateful for Medjugorje, and for what it did for me.

MEDJUGORJE—YOUTH—FR. KEN ROBERTS

Fr. Ken Roberts—Florissant, Missouri

One of the more striking elements of conversion in reference to Medjugorje is not just persons, but age groups. This is especially true of youth. Their presence in Medjugorje is constant and the fruits are very obvious.

Perhaps no single American priest has been more involved with youth in respect to Medjugorje than Fr. Ken Roberts. Over the years he has made dozens of pilgrimages to Medjugorje, always with great numbers of young people in tow. He can speak not only of conversions, but vocations as a result. In a letter to the Riehle Foundation in May of 1992, he had this to say:

"Medjugorje was a changing point in my priesthood. I renewed and revitalized my faith, especially in the Blessed Mother. I have made twenty visits to this small village in the last six years, almost always accompanied by youth. They travel there out of curiosity or because their parents see it as a last hope for conversion.

"Priests usually are the most cynical when it comes to believing in such manifestations. They ask, 'What if it is condemned, or what if it is a hoax, won't you look silly?' I answer them, 'In no way will I look silly since I have become closer to God through my visits and I am teaching NOTHING that is not already taught by the Church (repentance, prayer, fasting, the Eucharist and Confession).' I do not need Medjugorje in order to proclaim that, but it certainly has brought this message alive to millions who might otherwise have missed it and remained unconverted.

"The punch line is: 'What if she really is appearing and telling the world, this is your last chance? What if she really is appearing and you have not converted?'"

A CHAPLAIN

Fr. Joseph P. Cain, O.F.C.

The number of people who are drawn to Medjugorje with a desire to pray, and the atmosphere of prayer which pervades the place are evidence of some special graces at work.

I was impressed with the visionaries. They are, after all, goat herders and they are giving us profound theology. It is reminiscent of the Galilean fisherman who preached Christ Crucified. What they tell us the Blessed Mother told them sounds very like what the Blessed Mother would say. I did not need to see the sun dance or have my rosary turn to gold to be able to accept what they were saying. I liked the emphasis put on the Mass, and the fervor with which the pilgrims assisted at the Holy Sacrifice.

* * *

A BISHOP COMMENTS

Bishop Michael D. Pfeifer, O.M.I.—San Angelo, TX

As the Church continues to study and reflect on the mysterious and supernatural happenings of Medjugorje, I can only offer my personal opinion. I am convinced that Mary is appearing at Medjugorje, and that she is calling us to a deeper union with Jesus Christ, and to the faithful living out of His gospel in our daily lives...each one according to his or her vocation. Mary does not bring a new command, but simply the one she gave centuries ago at Cana, *Do whatever He* (Jesus) *tells you.*

Mary comes back today at Medjugorje as a kind and loving mother, pleading with our world...with all of us...to simply do what Christ tells us to do. If we listen to her gentle command, Christ, through the Holy Spirit, will work new and wonderful signs of grace and love in our individual hearts, in our families, in our communities, in the entire world.

THE REAL PRESENCE

Rev. John Cordaro—Scranton, Pennsylvania

At first I was touched by the spirituality of the village, but not by the commercialism and noisy movements, especially of the English speaking pilgrims and their priests, many of whom disregarded the sanctity of the place—attired in secular clothing—and reduced the Holy Sacrifice of the Mass to an element of entertainment and loud, boisterous outbursts, even during the Liturgy. I did complain to the Pastor, Fr. Orec, and he told me he tries to do the best he can to control the various pilgrim groups. I too was part of the above scene at first. Then gradually, after a few more trips to Medjugorje, I saw, as it were, the Light.

What really is the message of Our Lady? You certainly won't find it in all those externals, nor sensational manifestations. It was located with all its silent beauty and awe, right there hidden in the tabernacle under the appearance of ordinary bread.

That is what converted me. My liberal attitude changed to a quite conservative one and precisely to preserve the Truth and Beauty of the Real Presence—"Alter Christus!" The Eucharist!

* * *

Fr. Jim Willig—Cincinnati, Ohio

Medjugorje is an international and inspirational retreat center for many thousands of pilgrims each year.

The greatest miracle that is occurring there every day is the conversion of peoples' lives as they experience the presence of Our Lord and Our Lady. I witnessed and experienced this myself.

MEDJUGORJE IS FOR PRIESTS

Fr. Anthony Sirianni—Somerset, New Jersey

My pilgrimage to Medjugorje is one that enhanced my priesthood and revitalized my love for Mary, which inspired me to be a priest. I was ordained a priest for the Diocese of Metuchen in May of 1989. I am currently a hospital chaplain and Associate Pastor.

I heard of Medjugorje in May of 1984 when a priest friend from Kansas had experienced a true conversion of heart during his stay in Medjugorje. It was then that I felt I was called to Medjugorje, but studies and formation for the priesthood prevented me from going at that time. In 1991 I was called by a travel agent who was planning such a pilgrimage. She had been there before, and she wanted me to be chaplain for 18 people. My initial reaction was that I couldn't take the time away from my ministry, but after much contemplative prayer and many rosaries, I felt that I was being called to Medjugorje.

After I agreed to go, I started to reflect on the retreats I had been on over the last six years. I attended a thirty-day Ignatius retreat and several eight-day retreats. This would be my eight-day retreat for this year. But this was not just another retreat! This was a conversion! As soon as I got to Yugoslavia, I felt different. My prayer was emphasized, my heart was opened and this incredible feeling of holiness came over me. Even though I had never been to Lourdes or Fatima (thus having nothing to which I could compare this feeling), I was taken aback by this feeling of holiness. I know that there are many well educated people in our society that put the Rosary down, but it is a contemplative and meditative way to God. It calms one down and allows one to focus.

The focus of Medjugorje is on the Eucharist. Many people within the group were excited about this and amazed. They came from different prayer experiences also—from traditional to charismatic and contemplative. It was fascinating to see how the different types of worship were respected and shared, especially when it came to Eucharist. All became one body. The other sacraments (such as Reconciliation) were so alive and such healing experiences. Celebrating and receiving the sacraments was so wonderful because people weren't just going through the motions, but hearts were opened. Grace was a gift of God and the sacraments were truly healing.

St. Augustine always mentioned in his writings that our hearts express our bodies and souls. Through this, one whole being is embraced and loved by our Savior, Jesus Christ. Isn't this truly the work of our Blessed Mother? From the very outset of our life on earth, which begins our faith, the mother is the first to embrace the child. As the child grows and develops, other things can take place. Today in our society, parents want to be their children's friends. But, when the topic of religion or Church comes up, parents turn into police because of their experiences. Some have been burdened with much pain. This attitude pollutes our Church.

I met a number of people from all over the world in Medjugorje. I was able to come to a conclusion: we need to return to the time when parents are parents and when children have the love of their parents. Today's children are pearls being devoured by society's valueless influence.

The message of Mary to the young people was primarily to: 1) pray the Rosary, 2) go to Confession, 3) attend Mass, 4) fast, 5) read the Bible. These five messages are at the root of conversion of hearts opened through Mary to Jesus. What sound theology! The easy way of prayer and conversion. "Pray for peace, my children, in the world and in families." The young men and women I met were so real and open that they felt they had changed.

It's very difficult to be a priest in the 90s, especially when religious brothers and sisters are hurting themselves. As my faith was growing in Medjugorje, I realized how many others are hurting. Whether that hurt is caused by society or Church, we can't ignore it, but we must risk by asking Our Lord for forgiveness, guidance and, most of all, healing. What better way to start this process than to go to the Mother of Jesus, who intercedes for us to her Son and through the Sacred Heart of Jesus, pours graces and blessings upon us and strengthens our parishes, places of work, Churches, schools and most especially our homes.

I came back to America touched by hearts that were hardened and were now opened. I loved my group of strangers, who now are as close as family. I have written to priests and people from all over the world and pray the Rosary every day for peace. I even love being a priest in a country where people are attacked everyday and ministry is not easy. The Cross of Jesus is one that I carry with joy in my life.

There are so many people who could share their stories, but as a priest, it's important to share. Be open to Jesus. Have your heart open to Mary, and she will bring you to Jesus and the world will be a better place—one of love and prayer.

Pray! Pray! Pray!

* * *

Bishop Gabriel Diaz de Cueva—Ecuador
Bishop Joseph Casale, Archbishop of Foggia, Italy

Bishop Gabriel Diaz (Ecuador), and Bishop Joseph Casale, Archbishop of Foggia, Italy, stated:
—"Medjugorje is an extraordinary thing which invites us to change our lives. No one can remain indifferent about it. We will return" (*Eco,* no. 74).

* * *

Bishop Paul Hnilica

(From a sermon on June 25, 1990, in Medjugorje):
—"Twenty million pilgrims, 22,000 priests, and about 100 bishops and cardinals without counting those who have come incognito. Certainly, they would have been noticed if anything did not go well [...]; if there were some danger for the faith, they would have intervened. Now then, they permit and they remain silent [...]. I say to the skeptics and to everyone: 'Come and see.' (*Eco,* no. 75).

I FELT CALLED TO GO

Fr. Stan Rataj—Chicago, Illinois

When I went to Medjugorje, it was sort of a last minute thing, but I felt called to go there. I had to rearrange some pretty important things that I had already scheduled. But somehow, Mary made it all happen. She even got me through the plane ride which is no small feat as I am terrified of flying. I went with a small group of people from my parish.

I can honestly say, it was one of the most wonderful weeks of my life. It was certainly the holiest. I have felt good after retreats, but that wears off after awhile. However, four years later, my pilgrimage to Medjugorje is still affecting my spirituality, my prayer and my devotion to the Rosary. As I think back upon my week there, the only sadness I feel is for the people who are suffering the brutality of the war now. I wish them peace.

* * *

POPE JOHN PAUL II

Msgr. Hnilica, a Czech bishop in exile, a friend of the Pope, reported this remark by John Paul II, who was questioned on the opportunity of going on a pilgrimage to Medjugorje:
—"If I were not the Pope, I would have been there a long time ago!"

Since then, Msgr. Hnilica has reported another remark by John Paul II, speaking to a group of doctors involved in the study of Medjugorje, on August 1, 1989:
—"Yes, today the world has lost the sense of the supernatural. In Medjugorje, many have looked for it and found it in prayer, fasting and confession."

(From *Nine Years,* The Riehle Foundation)

DEEP CONVERSION

Fr. John Izral—New Orleans, Louisiana

It was my privilege to travel to Medjugorje with other pilgrims three times from 1989 through 1990. From the first time I read about the apparitions there, I always believed them genuine. But I put off going because I always felt others needed the experience more than I did.

When I finally went to Medjugorje, I experienced much more than I expected. I realized that most people didn't go to Medjugorje because they wanted to see Mary, or to experience something supernatural. Instead, they seemed to go because they had so much pain and hurt spiritually, emotionally, or physically, and they felt that here they would finally get some relief.

My greatest experience in Medjugorje was in hearing confessions and praying with people. I have never experienced anywhere, more powerfully, the charismatic gift of word of knowledge. I often cried along with the pilgrims as I felt their pain and hurt over some long ago incident that needed their forgiving or letting go as the Holy Spirit confronted them with it.

I have no quarrel with those whose rosaries changed color, or who saw the cross on Mt. Krizevac spin like a top, or who watched the sun dance or pulsate. But seeing deep conversions and lives transformed were for me the most powerful sign of the supernatural.

What do I feel now in 1992 about Medjugorje since my thoughts and feelings have matured and congealed? I think I would summarize them in the words of Ivan the visionary at the New Orleans Conference in 1990. He said: "We are now experiencing the dawn of the peace Mary promised at Fatima in 1917."

WHY DO YOU COME HERE?

Fr. Svetozar Kraljevic, O.F.M.—Medjugorje

This is not an everyday experience. For many, it is not the first time. For others, it is a new and unique experience. So let us reflect on what the purpose of pilgrimage is and what it is meant to accomplish. Listen to your heart and mind, to what they are telling you. You can trust them.

A pilgrimage is a mirror to see yourself, not others (that would be a tour). Jesus spoke of pilgrimage when He said *...who has given up home, brothers or sisters, mother or father, children or property, for Me...and persecution besides...will receive everlasting life (Mk.* 10:29-30). You have left home and country, brothers and sisters, to come here. You have suffered persecution besides: plane delays, lost baggage, money spent.

By accepting these sacrifices, you allow yourself to learn that you have so many other brothers and sisters you did not know you had. You all become brothers and sisters, for you all share the same experiences and are all in the same boat.

Pilgrimage is like a school: you learn about yourself, the meaning and the purpose of your life.

The devil, however, wants to divert you from your purpose. The devil uses his power to urge us to build our kingdom here on this earth. The message of Our Lady is the contrary; it is love, to learn to share with those in need.

Human abilities and possibilities, gifts and talents, are all given us to create order and peace and beauty in the world. But the devil tries to turn the best into the worst. And sadly, we often let the devil possess these gifts of holiness. Humanly speaking, we cannot do anything about it. Mary does not offer us an escape. She tells us to be aware of the devil and to pray. Our Lady's plan is simple: pray! God will do the rest.

Pray that God brings order into your lives. We do not have to think too much, to run around too much. We need simply to pray. Pray daily. Pray the way you know how. Pray that God helps you not to make the wrong moves, not to let the devil use your powers and abilities to further his own ends.

Prayer is a courageous thing to do. It is not easy. It is not compatible with our contemporary thinking, for prayer does not earn money, it does not entertain, it does not offer rest and recreation. Prayer does not make sense to the world. It is just the opposite of the world. Our Lady does not ask you to be perfect in prayer. It is not full of high experiences. She just says, "Pray." Take the rosary every day. Go to your neighbor. Be a good neighbor.

Our pilgrimage is a mirror to see ourselves—a courageous search for our soul. It is a look into our past. Recall the last five years of your life; the places where you have been. Look at your check stubs and see what you spent your money on. Am I comfortable with all this? Am I happy with what I have done? Was it a way to happiness?

You are not here to see the seers or sights. You are here as pilgrims, to search for God, to see Him face to face, that He may take your hand and lead you day by day.

God will give each one at Medjugorje the experience he needs. So many come hoping to find peace. We must not look to the things outside us, but to the heart within us. The problems are not outside us, but inside us. Look to your heart; do not be a reactor!

You are called to conversion here. At first it is exciting, joyful, like falling in love. But then the honeymoon is over. Conversion is like driving a car because every turn is a temptation and every oncoming car is a danger. Therefore, you must be alert. Drive carefully, for the devil seeks to smash you up. Drive constantly, prayerfully, for you must go on.

People come two or three times to Medjugorje. Each time they must get new graces. If you buy a pair of pants for a child, it won't fit him a year later. He grows. So you must search for deeper meaning and growth each time you visit Medjugorje. In marriage, one grows in the knowledge and acceptance of each other. Similarly, we must grow in heart and mind. God does not allow us to stay in the same place.

What should you do for Medjugorje?
Nothing, but be holy. That is the best we can do. God is calling us to this. He needs us all for Himself. Seek out the reasons, in your mind, why you came here.

THE EFFECT OF MEDJUGORJE ON ONE PRIEST

Fr. Richard Beyer—Burlington, Iowa

Medjugorje has had the greatest impact on my life since my ordination to the priesthood. My first trip was in November of 1987. It was then that I first experienced the Miracle of the Sun (a gift which has remained ever since), the rosaries that change to bright gold, seeing the three flashes of light that precede Our Lady's apparition to the visionaries, and witnessing the conversion and profound love of God which affected every member of my pilgrimage group. On subsequent trips I would witness a miraculous physical healing, speak in tongues for the first time, receive the charismatic gift to slay in the Spirit, and receive a mental-spiritual healing myself.

One of the greatest joys of Medjugorje has been to witness Our Lady confer these gifts on others as well. Of the dozen or so pilgrimages I have led, there has never been a member of any group who has not received extraordinary graces from the Madonna.

Why this outpouring? I feel it is for the same reason miracles accompanied the life of Jesus Himself: to authenticate His ministry as from God and to show forth His love for all the world to see. This is the modus operandi of the Holy Spirit. Rather than belittle or deemphasize the miraculous at Medjugorje, perhaps we should simply accept it as the gratuitous gift it is. As St. Paul says, *Rejoice in the Lord always. I say it again, rejoice!*

Hearing confessions in Medjugorje has also been an unforgettable experience. Never have I seen more repentance *and* joy, more sincerity and courage. There is no doubt in my mind that the Spirit of God is working in a special way in that little village so close to the heart of the Virgin.

There is an excitement over faith in Medjugorje that I have rarely seen before. People are aglow with the Spirit, full of kindness and the wonder of God's love. It is, sadly, a far cry from the staid practice of faith that we see in many parishes. The good news is that having been enlivened in their faith in Medjugorje, pilgrims return to their home churches and bring this new life with them. Thanks be to God, it is contagious.

My experience in Medjugorje culminated in 1991-1992, when

I was granted a leave from Diocesan work to finish a book I had been writing on the messages of Medjugorje. I was able to spend a few months in residence there—an unforgettable experience. The result was *"Medjugorje: Day by Day"* (to be published by Ave Maria Press in the summer of 1992), which is a series of reflections for each day of the year using the Madonna's messages tied in with Sacred Scripture. The inspiration and credit for the book lies primarily with Our Lady.

The meaning of Medjugorje? A new age of peace has dawned for mankind, but, as Our Lady says, "not through the politicians," but through grace and prayer. And all of us who have helped Our Lady through prayer, fasting, and sacrifice; all of us who have tried to live her messages; and all of us who have believed in her and trusted her—we too have had a part in ushering in this new age.

In decades to come historians will puzzle over the cataclysmic events of the 1980's and 90's and try to figure out how it could all have happened: the fall of the Berlin Wall, the liberation of Eastern Europe, the collapse of Communism, the rebirth of the Russian republics, the victory of both democracy and the philosophy of human rights. And most will be unaware that it was the work of a young maiden on a hillside in Yugoslavia, who wept for peace. Gathering the faithful from every land, she worked miracles. She continues to this day.

I BELIEVE

Fr. Gerald Ruane, Ph.D.—Newark, New Jersey

I was blessed to be on sabbatical during 1989-90; and in the eight months from the beginning of November to the first week of June, I went to Medjugorje four times. Each pilgrimage was a blessed experience; each one was quite different.

The first time I went I was really completely unaware of the impact that Medjugorje would have on me. I went with some skepticism, yet with a relatively open mind, to see a renewed parish. I did see that, but I saw something more. I came back a believer, but I don't think I really appropriated the message. It did not become a part of my daily life.

In February I went for a personal retreat which was a blessing and moved me closer to acceptance, but not completely. I did begin praying all fifteen decades of the rosary and doing some of the other things our Lady recommended. I was giving out medals and rosaries from Medjugorje, but in some way I was still, especially with other priests, acting the cool, clerical, impartial observer. I wanted to protect my reputation and my self-respect. After all, I wouldn't want anyone to think I was a religious fanatic, would I?

After my third pilgrimage, I realized my mixed motives, and it suddenly dawned on me that I truly believed that our Lady was appearing at Medjugorje. Whether every message was translated accurately, whatever the outcome of the dispute between the diocesan bishop and the Franciscans, I believe that our Lady is appearing there and that the messages are accurate to the largest extent. (From *Thank You For Hearing My Call*, Sacred Heart Press)

ONE WEEK IN JUNE, 1987

Fr. Alfred R. Pehrsson, C.M.

When one hundred of us from the Buffalo Diocese visited Medjugorje as a way of beginning the Marian Year in June of 1987, we journeyed with open minds and hearts. We weren't looking for "signs." We weren't desiring to receive "revelations." We just wanted to be in an apparently special place where we could celebrate the Liturgy and Sacraments with our Catholic international family such as the Italians, Austrians, Germans, Irish, English, Yugoslavians, among the many other nationalities. If "signs" were given to us on a few occasions, great! But as matured Catholics we knew the real moments of grace would be taking place in our hearts and souls. The Catholic unity, joy, love, solidarity and peace were those spiritual fruits that we had already experienced in such places as Lourdes and Fatima. Now we longed to experience them again, but this time in a communist country where Our Lady allegedly has been appearing since June 1981.

We met Maria Pavlovic and spoke to her for twenty-five minutes, thanks to our interpreter, Father Chris Coric, a Croatian-American priest. I was amazed at her serenity and humility. If I had to encounter daily so many repetitious and often frivolous questions as she has had to do for these past years, without a special supernatural assistance from Our Lord, I think I would have ended up in a Zagreb "Funny Farm" by this time.

Observing her innocence, her heroic generosity and sincerity, I thought of the guilt I would have if, on my false words, millions would bear annoying hardships in coming to this "end-of-the-world" countryside. My guilt would overwhelm me if I knew that because of my false messages thousands would climb a dangerous and rocky mountain path to the top of Mt. Krizevac (1,700 feet high), knowing the possibility of many people falling and injuring themselves on this treacherous path. On our own ascent to the mountain top, we met thirty Italians descending the rocky path. Ten of these adventurous people were blind. They stopped their singing long enough to greet us in their best English. It was a happy moment for us all.

My Philadelphia doctor marveled at the fact that with no cartilage in my knees (femur bones just rubbing on tibia bones), I effortlessly and painlessly climbed that steep, rocky, mountain path with my parishioners. I might not call it a "miracle," but I thank God for the opportunity to have arrived at a very special mountain cross.

After a thirty-priest concelebrated Mass one morning at 10:00 a.m., Father Benjamin introduced himself. He hailed from New Orleans, La. This was his second visit. Dressed in cassock and collar, he said to me, "Father Al, I know something very special and spiritual is happening here." Pointing to the hundreds outside the church of St. James, he continued, "Do you see these good people? Among them are priests, incognito, dressed in lay clothing. I have been experiencing a fantastic phenomenon for the past two weeks. It's just as if a sign visible only to priests has been hanging over my head...like a neon sign flashing, "I hear priests' confessions." So many have come to me, some in broken English, asking, 'Father, please hear my confession. I am a priest, a burned-out, tired priest. I need a renewal. I need to feel like a priest again. I need a good confession. And so we go aside from the crowds. They humbly kneel on the grass or stone pavement. They pour out their hearts. More than one has told me, 'I came to Medjugorje as a last resort. As they go away we happily embrace and I know Our Lord and Our Lady have shared these moments with us. This seems to be my special mission in this blessed place."

At 7:00 in the evening, thirty priests concelebrated the Croatian Mass on the eve of Pentecost Sunday before an overflowing congregation. Between loudly sung Croatian songs, there was silence so intense that at times I had to look up to see if everyone but a few neighboring priests had left the church. It was a devotional quiet. Later, as we priests returned from our assigned communion posts spread throughout the body of the church, my eyes watered and my throat "lumped" when the thousands thundered out "The Battle Hymn of the Republic" substituting "Alleluias" for the English words. Solidarity in its greatest yet simplest form! It is most evident here that the Mass is central to the Medjugorjian experience. Jesus Christ is central to the experience. The Madonna points to her Son and repeats the urgent message of John the Baptist, *"Repent! Reform your lives. The Kingdom of God is at hand. Behold the Lamb of God."* The message is repeated over and over in a thousand different ways. People are listening, maybe for the first time in many years.

As a Vincentian pastor I have many people under spiritual direction. With holy fear and trepidation do I counsel them, fully aware of my own accountability before the Lord as St. Paul reminds pastors. These Franciscans of Medjugorje must have the same pastoral and delicate conscience in regard to all their spiritual children, not only the "seers." If, as one ancient spiritual writer speculated, "The floor of Hell is paved with the skulls of priests" (those consecrated ones who in life were unfaithful to their priestly calling), then I am confident that these Franciscans have been superconscious of this reality. Any deliberate fraud and dastardly manipulation of events in this valley of Medjugorje would place them in grave sin and surely make them spiritually unbalanced. The very thought of appearing before an all-knowing God, Whose wrath is enkindled against false shepherds who mislead their flocks, is a frightening one.

After hearing confessions outside St. James' Church at 5:00 p.m. on June 6, a nurse from Buffalo whispered to me, "Father Al, look at the sun." My immediate thought was not of Jesus or Mary or "a trick of Satan," but of the overwhelming power of a loving heavenly Father, the Creator, Who was so smart that He had superimposed a huge "mother of pearl" disk over the heavenly body so we all could admire it. When we were kids we had "angel hair" that enhanced the colored Christmas tree lights. Angel hair seemed to surround our Medjugorje sun while brilliant and soft lights of red, blue, pink, purple, green flared out, danced and spewed forth from the throbbing circumference of the great mother of pearl white ball. "How great is our God..." And for one full hour many of us looked at that pulsating, magnificent heavenly phenomenon (so similar to the Fatima "Miracle of the Sun" in 1917).

I have a rosary blessed in Medjugorje by the Queen of Peace (and at her insistence by priests as well). Two years ago I showed it to a prayer group in Niagara Falls. A young father, Tony Sr. had been very much concerned about his four-year-old boy who was suffering from alopecia, total loss of body hair. He had taken little Tony to many area doctors. The verdict was that there was no cure. Self-consciously, the bald-headed child would wear a baseball cap to Sunday Mass.

Having seen the crude cord and marble rosary at the prayer

group, Tony Sr. asked if he could borrow it for a week. That very night he went home and as the child slept, Tony and his wife Mary prayed this rosary for a healing through Our Lady's intercession. They prayed the rosary faithfully every night. Soon blond hair started to grow on the child's bald head. Tony Sr. chuckled, "Blond hair on a little Italian-American kid. It looks great." Today the child has a full head of thick, black hair. The doctors have no medical answers. Let's just say with gratitude that it is a marvelous thing that today a six-year-old doesn't have to go through a child's purgatory, those sometimes cruel tortures that fellow classmates can inflict upon a bald or afflicted classmate. Tony wears a baseball cap now only to play baseball.

* * *

Fr. Liam Lawton—Dublin, Ireland

When one travels on pilgrimage through the mountainous regions of Herzogovina, one becomes conscious that he is soon to enter the village of Medjugorje: In one respect, a disappointment—a little place with two mountains and a church—but for him who looks more deeply, a place of great hope, a "window to Heaven." Aside from all the mantraps of modern entrepreneurship, which is infiltrating into this haven of peace too, there is here a great "school" providing the experience of peace, to build a new world. For many, the journey begins here, and it can last the whole life long. With hope, many will begin the journey in 1990 through "Youth 2000"...(from *Medjugorje,* July 1991).

FROM THOMAS TO TIMOTHY

Fr. Tim Deeter—Orangefield, Texas

Eighteen months ago I did not believe in Medjugorje at all. I was rather opposed to it, although I did allow people in my parish to speak to one another about it, to come to church and pray the rosary, and I knew that a few were going to Medjugorje. Some of the people in my parish gave me videos to watch (which sat on my TV set, unused, for over two years), magazines and articles to read (which I never read).

I finally gave in and decided to go to Medjugorje. Why? Because some of my teenagers went and they came back changed. They were asking to come into the church on weekday afternoons to pray the rosary. I knew that was not normal. I taught high school for fourteen years. I know what kids do and don't do. At CYO meetings they would talk about Medjugorje and sometimes be reduced to tears. I said, "This is really difficult for me to accept. I'm afraid these kids are going to freak out on me religiously and go through some big religious high and then hit a low point and perhaps leave the church all together." And so, as a pastor, I felt it my responsibility to go and see for myself before I passed a judgment that would be uninformed.

I was not convinced that Mary was appearing in Medjugorje, although I believed that she could—I believe in Fatima, in Lourdes, I'm not anti-Mary, I've always carried a rosary, I have Marian devotions. When I became a pastor in my parish, I consecrated the parish to the Blessed Mother. I was not a radical priest—anti-devotions, anti-Mary—but I just had my doubts because of the things I had read about the messages and about the length of the appearances and so many other theological points that people have raised.

As I was leaving, I decided to use the time-honored method of testing God. On the plane in Houston, as we were taking off, I said, "God, if Your Mother is truly appearing in Medjugorje, I want You to give me a sign by sending me someone there that will tell me a secret that only You and I know."

We arrived in Medjugorje after that wonderful 32 to 36 hour trip! Right away I was turned off. In the morning we got up to go to the 10 o'clock English Mass, and as I was walking with a group of people that I traveled with (not my parishioners—they had gone on a separate trip at the same time so that I would not prejudice them and they would not prejudice me) we saw a bunch of teenagers kneeling on the front steps of St. James Church, praying the rosary, cross-style. These adults with me were saying, "Isn't it wonderful to see teenagers praying in public like that and praying with such devotion and discipline?" As we came closer, I saw that they were my teenagers, from my parish! I was proud of them, but I thought to myself, I didn't have to travel to Yugoslavia to be proud of my teenagers.

I concelebrated the Mass with about fifty other priests. It was great, the singing was wonderful, and the responses were whole-hearted. It was a wonderful Eucharist, but I thought to myself, I don't have to travel to Yugoslavia to experience a great Eucharist with a lot of priests and a lot of people who really believe.

I climbed Apparition Hill and I led our group of pilgrims in prayers, although I hadn't the faintest idea of what Apparition Hill was all about. I just made the prayers up and went through the motions. Priests are very good at that at times—we're in the business of praying, you know, and sometimes it does become more of a business than a prayer. I was not moved at all.

After supper that evening they said, "We're going to Mass again." I said, "Again?" I took a book by Thomas Merton along to read, and I didn't intend to concelebrate. In fact, I traveled in civilian clothes. I did not go as a priest, I did not want to be bothered as a priest. So I sat outside the church on the benches, the way so many people do because of the overflow crowds. Mass began and it was broadcast on loud speakers to the people outside. When the readings began, I didn't understand a word, so I went back to reading my book. When the Gospel was read and the homily was preached, I began listening. As I was listening, I began to realize that I was understanding. And not simply a vague under-standing of the general message, but I was understanding every word that was being said in Croatian. I began to think, "My God, this is what happened at Pentecost when people from all over the world of many races and languages gathered together to hear the word of God, and they heard it, each in his own language." And in talking with people in confession and in counseling, I have found that I have not been the only one to experience that Pentecost event.

The next day, Thursday, was the traditional feast of Corpus Christi. Our group was going to get up early in the morning to go to a nearby village called Tihaljina to hear a priest, named Fr. Jozo preach. I did not know who this man was and I said, "We have come all this way, we're finally here in Medjugorje, there are priests crawling all over the place, now we're going to get up in the dark, early in the morning, get on another bus, go to another town, listen to another priest talk? Can't we leave well enough alone?" But, being the good priest that I am, not wanting to be the only one to stay in bed, I got up and went very begrudgingly to Tihaljina.

During the rosary, out came this priest. When he began to speak, I realized that he was the priest who had spoken the night before in Medjugorje, the priest I could not see because he was in the church and I was outside. It was Fr. Jozo. He offered a beautiful homily and a beautiful meditation on Medjugorje, and I whispered over to my guide, "I would really like to talk to this man sometime." I thought nothing more of it. After Mass we all went up to be blessed by Fr. Jozo. As he began to bless people I saw some of them slain in the Spirit, falling over on the ground. I had never seen this before. I had heard about it, I knew about it, but I had never seen it—and I was scared! I saw some of my teenagers, who I knew very well, hit the floor so fast that I knew that something was happening there, and I was scared as he came around the circle, moving his way toward me. I said, "My God, he's some sort of charismatic." I knew what "charismatic" meant, which made it all the scarier for me. As he got to me, he put one hand on my head and one hand on the head of the man next to me, (I was in civilian clothes), and he prayed over me and I bit my tongue, and I kept saying over and over in my heart, "God, I don't want this to happen." Nothing happened! He walked on and I was relieved.

He came right back! I had one of those buttons on that said "Mir Retreat—Fr. Tim Deeter." He pointed to the name "Tim" and said, "Teem." And I know he meant, "What does that mean?" So I spoke the only language I felt I could communicate with him in, I spoke in Latin. 'Timotheus.' And I said in Latin, "I am a priest." And he said, "Ah, Timotheus." He put both hands on my head, and I felt such warmth go through my body, from my head to my feet. I didn't get slain—I wouldn't allow it.

Well, I felt very good about the Tihaljina experience; I was glad it was over, but it was interesting. I chalked it up as a good experience.

Then we went back to Medjugorje for another Mass that evening. Mass, Rosary, Mass, Rosary!! It was Corpus Christi, as I said, and they were planning a special Mass, a big Mass, lots of incense and a long procession outside the church. I was interested in that because I have always heard about those beautiful expressions of faith in Europe. This time I decided to go as a priest and get my seat up front.

The next day, I gave in, I surrendered. I spent the entire day, from 8:30 in the morning until 10:30 that night, hearing confessions, with only a half-hour break in the evening for supper. It was the best day of my priesthood! I loved it! I used to wonder how St. John Vianney could spend 12 to 18 hours a day in the confessional. Now I know that it was not so much a burden as a real experience of faith for him, because what happened to me was person after person, from all over the world, had come to me telling me that God is there in Medjugorje, that God is moving hearts to conversion, that God is changing hard hearts, especially priests.

On Saturday, the following day, and again on Sunday, I saw the sun pulsating. I saw a man who was crippled and in a wheelchair get up and walk, and at that point none of this astounded me, because I realized that whenever people are gathered together in great numbers, as Jesus said.. "I am there." And I took it for granted then, that the greatest miracle of all in Medjugorje is not the external things that we look at—the rosaries changing to gold, the photographs that people have, even the healing miracles—the greatest miracle of all is that in Medjugorje, in one place in the world, Christians were doing what Jesus had asked us to do 2,000 years ago. Christians were praying together, singing together, loving together, healing together, giving together and forgiving together. People often say now that Rome is the *head* of the Church, but Medjugorje is the *heart* of the Church.

On Monday I had learned that my group leader had arranged for me to meet with Fr. Jozo privately. There were a number of delays—by the time I got there I was four hours late for my appointment. Not a very good first impression! As I arrived, Anka, his translator, came up to me and said, "Father only has a few minutes to speak with you, so whatever you have to say, say it fast and don't delay him."

I went to the rectory and waited in the entrance hall and he came in. With arms outstretched he said to me in Italian, "Tommaso" which means Thomas. I said to him, "No, Father, my name is Timothy." He smiled and said, "No. You came here 'Thomas' (the doubting disciple), you leave here 'Timothy,' (which in Greek means 'he who fears the Lord'). I then said, "I am the pastor of those young people that you liked so much." (Pastor means 'shepherd.') Fr. Jozo again smiled and said, "Ah, yes, the sheep led the shepherd here. Now the shepherd must go home and lead the sheep." Then he took me by the shoulders and whispered into my ear the secret I asked God to reveal to me as a sign that His Mother is present in Medjugorje—in the very words I had planned on the plane in Houston. I looked at him in shock, and I think it was at that moment that I was slain in the Spirit. I just fell to the floor and the life of Jesus flashed before my eyes, and I saw all these Gospel incidents of Jesus healing people and forgiving people, and I realized that Fr. Jozo is a special witness of the life of Christ—healing and forgiving. That's what all priests are supposed to be. Our business is not building and running businesses, but our business is healing and forgiving and sharing the word of God. I finally said, "Father, I am a great sinner, but I want to be a good priest and a holy priest." I had never before thought of those words, that my aim in life should be becoming a holy priest. He lifted me up and said, "Sorry, I have to go to Medjugorje, but Anka, my interpreter, will tell you the things I was going to tell you."

She told me many things that are just beginning to be revealed to me and allowed to be revealed to others. She spoke, as she cried, describing Fr. Jozo's imprisonment, and the sufferings he endures even now. She told me, "Fr. Jozo is well aware that your parish is a little Medjugorje too, that it is small and rural, that its people are simple but devout, that they love Our Lord and Our Lady. He is aware of the fact that you promote devotion to the Blessed Sacrament and to the Blessed Mother. He is especially pleased that you work with the young directly and not through delegates, that you are trying to lead your people to more frequent confession. He said you must return to your parish now and announce Our

Lady's messages to them. Ask them to listen to her words with great love; to pray, especially the Rosary, every day; to fast, if possible, on bread and water every Wednesday and Friday; to confess their sins every month; to live together in peace; and to change their way of living. Father says your parish has a special mission to pray for American priests who are so often weak in faith and in devotion to their sacred duties."

She also told me something that I only recently revealed to my parish. "Fr. Jozo tells you to remember always that of all the people in your parish, you are the one charged with the special responsibility of preparing your people for the coming of Jesus Christ. A great cloud is descending upon the Catholic Church in America. There are many people who are disloyal to the Holy Father and to the teaching authority of the Church, and without knowing it, they are preparing for a schism. People in America will have to decide whom they will follow. Father, you must form your people in the truth of the Catholic faith and make your people strong so that your church will be a refuge for all those who will need a place to go where they can be Catholics."

I asked her, "Does Fr. Jozo see the Blessed Mother himself?" And she whispered, "Yes, frequently, perhaps even daily." I realized that many of the things he said to me were not his words, but Our Lady's words.

Our parish began, as a group, to live the messages of Medjugorje, based simply upon the word of their priest, which shows again the importance that priests play in the lives of their parishes. If they will speak from their hearts a message of conversion and faith, the people are ready to hear it.

I would say this to you, the lay people: do not go to your priest showing them rosaries that have turned gold or photographs of supernatural visions. Priests are not impressed by that. Priests need a whole different approach, because those things turn priests off. It turned me off. I'm still not impressed with rosaries turning gold—when mine does maybe I'll be impressed. Show your priests your conversion of life. Do not get angry with your priests because they do not accept the message; do not speak against them behind their backs or to their faces. Be patient with them the way my people were with me. I found out that my people were praying for me to go to Medjugorje—for three and one-half years they prayed!

We priests need the support of our people to help our faith grow, not by looking at your rosaries, but by looking at your faces in constant attention during Holy Mass as we show you the Body and Blood of the Lord Jesus. We need to hear your sincere confessions of your own sins, not your blame of everybody else in your family and at work for your troubles, but your outright acknowledgment—"I am a sinner and I need forgiveness." And we need to witness your spirit of sacrifice and service. The fast that God desires most of all is a life lived out of love for others. That and only that is going to change the hearts of priests and bishops.

Every parish is called to pray for American priests. Every parish is called to prepare each other for the coming of Jesus Christ. It's going to come some time—it may be a million years from now, but it might be tonight, and we must be ready.

There truly is a God, He truly exists. He knows each one of us by name, whether it's Thomas or Timothy. He knows what we're doing as sheep or as shepherd. He calls each one of us to a special task—through Mary, His Mother, leading us to Jesus, His Son—to accept our own part in His plan, whatever our part may be. It must be done, as St. John the Baptist recommended at the beginning of Jesus' ministry, with humility and a consciousness of our sins. It must be done as Jesus the Obedient Servant did, with prayer and with fasting. It must be done as Paul did, with faith in the one true God. It must be done as Mary did, with the spirit of total self-surrender—*I am the servant of the Lord. Let it be done to Me according to Your word.* And it must be done, people of God and my brother priests, *today* and not tomorrow, because tomorrow may be too late.

We, too, may be humbled and brought to our knees for our sins in this nation. We must never forget that if God exists He is not only good, but He is just. He will call us each to account; especially His priests will be called to account for what we are doing to and for our people. *"Stay awake, therefore. You do not know the day nor the hour of His coming."* And He has sent His Mother to prepare us! (From a talk in New Orleans, Dec. 1991)

45

FR. EMILIANO TARDIF, M.S.C.
Missionary of the Sacred Heart from the Dominican Republic

I often say to people that you have to judge the tree according to its fruit. And the fruits of Medjugorje are so numerous—people who have been converted, who have begun to live a Christian life after coming to Medjugorje. Therefore, this cannot be due to imagination. Neither can this be from the devil. There is one explanation that one must seek. And the Virgin, the Mother of God—as Pope Paul VI said in the document on evangelization—is the star of our evangelization...And I believe that the Mother of God is simply there in Medjugorje to call the Gospel back to memory for us. She has come, in order to read the Gospel to us once again, in order to evangelize us. People must accept the reality that the Mother of God is in Heaven with her glorified body, and she can appear with her glorified body. This is a dogma of the faith in the Catholic Church, the doctrine of the Assumption of Mary into Heaven. (From *Medjugorje,* July, 1991.)

* * *

PRAY, PRAY, PRAY!
Fr. Joe Galic, O.F.M.

Many years have gone by since we started listening to Mary's messages at Medjugorje. She emphasizes that she is calling us to live the messages. In her message of July 25, 1989, she urged us to *Renew your hearts, open yourselves to God and surrender to Him all your difficulties and crosses, so that God may turn everything into joy.*

Our Lady never forces us, but she repeatedly urges us to give God our time, like true children of God. God the Father has given us all the time that we have; He has given us our lives, each moment of them. Prayer means giving some of that time back to Him, giving Him as much as we can. Our words are not important in prayer. Rather, in silence we give Him time, and invariably, our hearts are renewed in this prayer. In prayer, our difficulties and crosses are turned into joy—but first we must make time to pray, time to be with God. (From *Heart of Medjugorje* October 1989.)

TESTIMONY OF BISHOP PAUL HNILICA

Paul Hnilica—Auxiliary Bishop of Rome
Titular Bishop of Rusoda

After my third visit in these places, I was able to arrange for a little more time to speak with the visionaries and also with the people who live close to them in everyday life. I wanted to examine and understand what reasons the one who talks against Medjugorje and is opposed to it had for doing so.

I am convinced that this is a case of slandering.

These children are not manipulated. They are simple and sincere. I see a supernatural aspect in these events. Morally, they force us to treat them very seriously. Upon my conscience, I must come to the conclusion that the voice of God is speaking with power at Medjugorje. Crowds of people go there to manifest by their piety their profound belief in those events.

Here at Medjugorje, something extraordinary is going on. Although these events are taking place in a country, small and not well known, they are happening within the Church and in the interest of all mankind.

We must not and we cannot take the gifts of God lightly.

(Translated from a quotation taken from *"Madre di Dio"*—1986/4.)

* * *

PILGRIM PRIEST DIES IN MEDJUGORJE

Fr. Julius S. Stefurosky—Pennsylvania

Fr. Julius S. Stefurosky (72) from Pennsylvania died suddenly at the 10 o'clock English-language concelebrated Mass on October 4, 1989—the feast of St. Francis of Assisi. Before the pilgrimage, he had said to friends: *"I'd like to go to Medjugorje and die there!"*

AN *ANGLICAN* REFLECTION ON MEDJUGORJE

Rev. C. Edward South, St. Andrew Episcopal Church—Mentor, OH

Anglicans, or Episcopalians as we are called here in America, are known for being the 'via media,' the middle road of Christianity. Unfortunately, what sometimes happens with such a position is that we are often found straddling the proverbial fence on many important issues.

So it is, I sense, with the Anglican position on Mary, the Mother of God.

On the one hand, we have liturgical references from Creeds and Eucharistic Prayers about the Virgin Mary; we have Eucharistic Prayers of the People, some of which conclude with a reference to our eventual inheritance with the Blessed Virgin Mary...and other saints. We sing or say the Magnificat, the Song of Mary, and our Collect for the Feast of the Visitation states, "Father in Heaven, by your grace the virgin mother of your incarnate Son was blessed in bearing him, but still more blessed in keeping your word...(Visitation 5/31)." Our Anglican parallel to the Roman Catholic Feast of the Assumption is the Feast of St. Mary the Virgin, whose Collect begins, "O God, you have taken to yourself the blessed Virgin Mary, mother of your incarnate Son: Grant that we, who have been redeemed by his blood, may share with her the glory of your eternal kingdom..." (St. Mary the V. 8/15).

Probably all Episcopalians would agree that if God, through the Archangel Gabriel, called Mary "the favored one," and if the early Church in Council determined Our Lady to be "The Mother of God"...then she really is something special.

But, what we *say* about Mary is not necessarily how we *behave*. It is acceptable as a Anglican, to have a *head* knowledge about her but not a devotional attitude. This may come out of centuries of misunderstanding about special devotions such as the Rosary, which is infrequently found, although not unknown among Anglicans. This is the heritage out of which I came as a cradle Episcopalian. My own spiritual journey always had a special place for Our Lady, but only that: a niche of reverence, a special feeling for her as Jesus' mother. That is, until Medjugorje.

I first heard of the apparitions in late 1984 and came across occasional references over the next few years...all of which sounded interesting and probably valid, but I took no special notice of them—until August of 1988.

My wife and my then 15-year-old-stepson went to Medjugorje. We had recently undergone a move from Alabama to a parish in northern Ohio and were experiencing all the appropriate trauma: our 8- and 9-year-old couldn't understand why we had to move at all; Paul missed his old friends and school as only teenagers can; the new parish and I were undergoing the usual transitional turmoil. Lee was trying to handle all of us!

When they returned from that trip, however, it was almost as if they were different people. They had a peace about them which was almost physical. The other children and I were the indirect beneficiaries of their visit, for our home became so filled with contentment that we could not help but be affected by it. The next summer, Lee and Paul again went to Medjugorje, with the same end result, peace and a real sense of direction for their lives.

Lee urged me to go the next year, but I said I would not go without her. I didn't know that she had been asking God to change my heart. And so He did: in the spring, I came home one day and announced my decision to to go Medjugorje with Paul in August. Reservations and visas were secured, and I was ready to go (without Lee). I casually mentioned to her that it would be great if she could come with us to Medjugorje. The younger children would have to be provided for, arrangements would have to be made for my 87-year-old-father, space on the pilgrimage would have to be available. All this seemed much too complex to ever work out in two weeks, but through a series of near-miraculous (read 'providential') events, the three of us made the August 1990 pilgrimage.

My first spiritual confrontation in Medjugorje had to do with my receiving Eucharist at St. James' Parish. I did receive and felt terribly convicted as the day wore on: a great sadness and depression set in, but it seemed to be very generalized and not uniquely focused on the question of receiving communion at a Roman Catholic altar. I began to ask myself the question: "Why am I here? What is the purpose?"

That Friday night we went up to Apparition Hill to be with Ivan's prayer group (along with thousands of other pilgrims). At the moment of our Lady's appearance, I saw three illuminating strobe-like, bluish-white flashes of light, and at the conclusion of the apparition a brilliant shooting star crossed the heavens. When I learned that not everyone sees the three flashes of light signifying Our Lady's appearance to the visionaries, I began to feel as though there might be a purpose to my being there...but, again, what was it?

On Sunday morning at 5:30, our group began to ascend Cross Mountain, making the Stations of the Cross on the way up. By the time we arrived at the top, I began to ask myself, "I say that I am sorry for my sins...but am I really? Is it all a 'head trip'—an intellectual exercise of repentance? Am I really sorry deep in my spirit?"

At the English Mass that day, I received the Eucharist spiritually...not the physical species of bread and wine from a priest, but the Body and Blood of Christ in a spiritual sense. This concept is familiar within Anglicanism as well as in Roman Catholicism.

At the Rosary that evening at St. James, I was still reflecting on these issues within me. As a part of my prayer offering, I specifically offered my doubts and my sins to Our Lady, to do with as she wanted! Suddenly, at the moment Mary appeared to the visionaries, I was overwhelmed with such a personal sense of sorrow that I began weeping uncontrollably. At the moment the Rosary resumed, signifying the end of the apparition, I stopped weeping completely. I had been blessed (touched by Our Lady) with an outward and visible sign of my contrition, to offset feelings that I was only superficially contrite.

I began to feel that going to confession would be a formal and sacramental acting out of my experience...but would a Roman Catholic priest hear an Anglican confession?

Early the next morning, a series of earthquake tremors awoke most of us pilgrims and many of the villagers. I took this somewhat jolting experience to mean that it would be a good idea to make my confession as soon as possible. The next day after Mass, and a wait of over an hour in line with others making their confessions, I entered the confessional and told the priest that I, an Anglican priest, knew he would not be able to give me absolution...but would he hear my confession? He did, and at the conclusion of my confession assured me of God's pardon and absolution. I left the confessional surrounded by a wonderful peace! The contrition of the prior night was completed in the outward and visible signs of confession.

Other moments of peace and insight continued during the week, concluding with my seeing the miracle of the sun...a truly awesome sign of God's presence in that place.

God's purpose in allowing Our Lady to come to Medjugorje has been very public from the start: to convert and reconcile the whole world to her Son, Jesus. This call for conversion demands a response, a decision from those who hear the message. A "yes," a "Let it be done to me according to your word," from the hearts of those who come to Medjugorje, or from those who hear of the messages, finds its reality in a new attention and commitment to prayer, fasting, daily Bible reading, monthly confession and (where available) daily Eucharist.

For Anglicans, this is nothing startling or new...it is what we should be doing all the time! But why is the excitement of Medjugorje not seen elsewhere? Why aren't Christians pushing and shoving to get into a church already jam-packed so they can participate in Eucharist? Why do we not experience a burning desire to confess our sins and receive the promise of absolution? What drives thousands and thousands of pilgrims to risk sprains, if not broken bones, to climb up and down Mt. Podbro and Mt. Krizevac at all hours of the day and night?

As others have pointed out, Medjugorje is both a school of prayer and a school of holiness. The students attending this school, the pilgrims, are gradually made aware of the Grace of God in this place: the gift of the Mother of God herself, who wishes to help us become more fully what we confess that we are in our various communions, be it Protestant or Anglican, Orthodox, Moslem, Jew or Roman Catholic. And that is one of the greatest miracles of Medjugorje, for this is *not* simply a Roman Catholic place, but an oasis of God's peace and love for the whole world. It is not without cost, not without personal sacrifice...but then, contrary to what the world would have us believe, there is no such thing as "cheap grace."

- I returned from Medjugorje with an inner peace beyond my wildest imagination: peace about my ministry, my family, my relationship with Jesus.

- I returned from Medjugorje with a deeper conversion to the Lordship of Jesus and also with a deeper appreciation of the role of Our Lady both in God's plans and in my private devotions.

- I returned from Medjugorje with a deeper sense of urgency for prayer and fasting, for personal confession and a deeper meaning of the Eucharist.

Addendum: We returned to Medjugorje in June of 1991 for the 10th anniversary of the apparitions.

* * *

A RETURN TO MEDJUGORJE

Fr. Jiri Gaberle

The renewal of Christian spirituality in the 1980s did not come from Rome, but from a little village in Yugoslavia—Medjugorje.

The people who return to Medjugorje, as I did, are not looking for outward manifestations of their religion, but for inward transformation of their lives. However, the same spirit is also with the people who experience Medjugorje for the first time.

A visit to Medjugorje touches people's lives. It might not be apparent immediately to outsiders, but those who visit Medjugorje know about it. People are hungry to be truly touched by God and not merely hear the words about God. The experience of being touched by God has to be lived and not only heard about. Most people are going to Medjugorje where they can experience God in a way they do not experience Him in their homes. (From *Catholic Herald,* Dec. 1989.)

TRANSFORMATION OF LIFE

Fr. Ron Roth—LaSalle, Illinois

Recently, I realized one of my life-long dreams—to visit Europe. And along with a tour of Germany, Austria and northwestern Yugoslavia, I led a group of pilgrims to Medjugorje.

Every day thousands of people stream by busloads, taxi cabs and on foot from all over the world to attend the three-hour services celebrated there.

I was strolling the grounds around the church late one afternoon with a member of our group. At one point, he told me that he could look directly into the sun and his eyes did not burn. I turned to look and was totally amazed. Suddenly, what looked like a whole wheat host appeared and covered the sun. I was awestruck. After a few seconds the host disappeared, and the sun began to pulsate, swirl and dance from right to left. When it stopped, I saw the figure of the kneeling Madonna on the left side of the sun. With that, I was brought to my knees by a peaceful force which overwhelmed me.

At that moment, hundreds of people began to fill the courtyard of St. James Church where we were standing. Some people were jumping up and down, others were kneeling with bowed heads, and a great number were crying. Tears began to stream down my face as I witnessed the awesome power of God. What else could it be?

I knew that it was not my imagination, because thousands of others have reported experiencing this and similar phenomena prior to this time. I had read of such reports in books about Medjugorje.

What a blessing it was to celebrate Mass in the room of the apparitions during the afternoon of the next day with the people who accompanied me on our journey of faith. Later that second evening, I again concelebrated the Eucharist at St. James with over 40 priests. The devotion of the thousands who participate in these three-hour services every night is extraordinary.

I can say without a doubt that this is the renewal Vatican II had desired in every parish throughout the world. This is what makes Medjugorje different from the appearance of our Blessed Mother at Lourdes and Fatima—the transformation of life. And this is what I feel is the greatest miracle occurring there.

There isn't room here to describe what this experience has done for me. It has strengthened my faith, expanded my joy and increased my desire to pray. In short, it has renewed my spiritual life. My life will never be the same again.

In total, I made four pilgrimages to Medjugorje and each one was a unique experience of the Holy Spirit's calling upon my life. I took the messages of Medjugorje seriously and preached them in my parish. The messages made a profound impact on my parishioners, as well as the many people who traveled many miles to attend the various religious/spiritual services that were offered on a weekly basis. These messages continue to make an impact on my personal life as well as my priesthood.

* * *

HE WANTS OUR ATTENTION

Fr. Jack Spaulding—Scottsdale, Arizona

Mary is here. She's not only in Medjugorje. She's here in Northfield, she's in Chicago, she's in Indianapolis, she's in Akron, Ohio, and yes, she's even in Scottsdale! But most of all she's in our hearts. She is our Mother; Jesus gave her to us...for so many different reasons. One of those reasons is to remind us of His love. One of those reasons is to remind us that He will never abandon us. One of those reasons is that He wants us to remember always that He knows us—He knows who we are.

Look at what's happened in Medjugorje. Those of us who have been there maybe went to find Mary, and we found Jesus. And if we found Mary, she took us by the hand and led us closer to Jesus. The focal point of Medjugorje is the Eucharist...not a Marian cult...but the Eucharist.

And so we don't need to go to Medjugorje. We have the Eucharist wherever we are. We have Reconciliation wherever we are. And we have Mary wherever we are.

It seems to me that whenever Jesus truly wants us to get our attention, He sends His mother. I think He really wants to get our attention! (From a homily given at Northfield, Illinois, June 1990).

54

A BISHOP FROM INDIA

Bishop Gratian Mundadan, C.M.I.—Bishop of Bijnor, India

Still another visit, I made, a visit to Medjugorje. That again was a great experience. I don't say anything about the apparitions of Our Lady there; the Church has not yet pronounced on it.

What impressed me was the crowds attracted to this place. And they come to PRAY and DO PENANCE. Hours and hours, without any fatigue or tiredness, they pray; day and night without any difference they climb the hill of apparition in prayer, meditating on the Passion of Our Lord. Their fervor left unforgettable impressions on me. I heard several stories of real conversion, spiritual awakening. Unwillingly, as like leaving the Holy Land, I returned to my diocese as my duty demanded me to come back. But I wanted to go again.

All this confirms my conviction that Our Blessed Mother has taken in her hands the task of converting the world to the Lord. It is the "Era of The Mother." (From *Our Lady Queen of Peace Prayer Group.*)

* * *

Bishop Sylvester W. Treinen, Bishop of Boise, Idaho

Msgr. Sylvester Treinen, Bishop of Boise, Idaho, USA, stated in his homily at the Conference at the University of Notre Dame (USA) on May 14, 1989:

"During our visit *ad limina,* I had 15 minutes of private conversation with the Pope. I told him then:
—I am just returning from Medjugorje. Some beautiful things are taking place there.

The Pope answered:
—Yes, it is good for the pilgrims to go to Medjugorje, to pray and to do penance. It is good.
It is first hand; I heard it with my ears."

RECONCILIATION

Fr. Raymond Favret—Cincinnati, Ohio

I have a strong devotion to Our Blessed Mother. I visited Fatima within a year of my ordination at the time when the present basilica was still under construction, and I have been back several times since. I have visited Lourdes, and also Knock when I was in Ireland, and I have been to Guadalupe several times. In addition to that, I was stationed in Washington, D.C. right on the grounds when the National Shrine of The Immaculate Conception was being completed.

I was therefore curious about Medjugorje, particularly after a number of parishioners in my former parish (Guardian Angels) had come back with impressive accounts of what had happened and how their faith was strengthened. My brother-in-law made a trip there and gave similar accounts. I was a little hesitant because of the negative attitude of the local bishop there, but I decided to go and find out for myself. So on a trip to Italy with another priest and my brother from Cleveland and his wife, we arranged to fly to Dubrovnik from Rome and spend several days at Medjugorje in October of 1990.

When I arrived in Medjugorje I was very disappointed to hear that the local bishop had forbidden the visionaries to be in church for the evening Mass when they usually had their visit from Our Blessed Mother. Naturally I was looking forward to being in the Church for that. At the same time, I was very pleased to hear the way the local Franciscans presented that decision of the bishop to the people. They did it in a very matter of fact and dignified way without any rancor or anything like that.

There are a lot of things I like about Medjugorje, but the one I would like to highlight here is the Confessions. My priest friend and I volunteered to hear confessions in English from 4:00 to 6:00 p.m. for two days. We wound up hearing until about 6:45 both days because people kept coming. But the number of confessions was not what impressed me as much as the quality of them. They weren't so much big sinners coming back, as good people wanting to grow much closer in their relationship to the Lord. They were people who had decided to make a change in their lives and were seeking help in doing it. For some of them, that was going to require real sacrifices and they were willing to face that.

In this sacrament I saw definite evidence that God was working through Mary in a very real way at Medjugorje.

*   *   *

Cardinal-Designate Urs Von Balthasar

Cardinal designate von Balthasar died suddenly several years ago, at the age of 82. His death came just two days before he was due to receive the red hat from Pope John Paul II. Von Balthasar was recognized as a giant figure in the world of theology and culture. Cardinal du Lubac hailed him as the most cultured mind of our generation. He was on very close terms with the likes of Cardinal Ratzinger, Fr. René Laurentin and Fr. Karl Rahner. His views on Medjugorje were expressed in sundry articles and letters, and he noted how pastorally wise and opportune was Our Lady's recommendation of monthly confession as the instrument to sanctify and renew the Church. In one article he stated:

"Medjugorje's theology rings true. I am convinced of its truth. And everything about Medjugorje is authentic in a Catholic sense. What's happening there is so evident, so convincing."

He also expressed his thoughts in much stronger language to Bishop Pavao Zanic of Mostar.

MARY'S TIME

Fr. R. Leroy Smith—Cold Spring, Kentucky

Before the war started in Croatia, I was fortunate enough to have made nine trips to Medjugorje between October, 1988 and April, 1991. There were over 650 pilgrims with me during these trips and all were spiritually renewed by the experience—I know I was!

On my first pilgrimage we landed in Dubrovnik in the late afternoon and took a three hour bus ride to Medjugorje. We arrived at about 8:00 p.m. Since there were no street lights in Medjugorje then, it was completely dark. If the tour guide hadn't announced that we were there, nobody would have known.

The 62 of us lodged in local peasants' homes. That was a memorable experience! We were all exhausted, but the lady of each house had something ready for us to eat. Out of politeness we all felt obliged to sit and eat. The lighting in that little house was so bad, I didn't know what I was eating. When I finally got to my room, it was so dark in there I couldn't even see the bed I was to sleep in. Imagine my surprise when I opened my suitcase and it was full of women's clothing. Relief came a few hours later when my luggage found its way to our little house. From then on I made sure I could identify my luggage easily. I thought I would freeze to death that night. I was never so cold in my life. But after finally falling asleep, from mere exhaustion, I awoke about 6:00 a.m.

It was a beautiful morning as I dressed and went outside the little house. I found my way to the Church of St. James, which reminded me of a cathedral in the wilderness, since there were no buildings around the church.

As I walked toward the church, there were a few makeshift buildings that I passed. Over the door of one, in English, was the sign "SUPER-MARKET." Inside were a few loaves of bread, some milk and a few meager other commodities. As I walked a little farther, another building had the sign reading, "EXPRESS-GRILL," and underneath it, "Hamburgers, Cheeseburgers, Coke." I surmised that in ten years it probably would be a McDonald's.

I finally arrived at the church. It was close to 7:00 a.m. and one of the early Masses was beginning—I think it was Italian. Afterward I discovered that Masses began in the church at 7:00 a.m. and followed one after the other in different languages. Our English Mass was always at 10:00 a.m. From that time on we (all the pilgrims) met at the church to plan our daily activities. The Mass was always the highlight of the day with thousands of people attending, both inside and outside the church. In the past three years I have had the privilege of being the main celebrant four times. Each was a remarkable experience of faith! No one has ever attended a more faith-filled Mass with such devotion to Our Lord in the Blessed Sacrament.

I like to recall my earlier experiences in Medjugorje, because they are my first impressions and most lasting of all my trips. So many wonderful things happened those five days. I met and talked to the visionaries—those simple, unassuming, humble young people to whom the Blessed Mother was appearing daily. I hiked up the Mountain of Apparitions and Cross Mountain. I was there while the apparitions in the church took place during the evening Rosary. I mingled with the townspeople who couldn't do enough for us. I saw rosary after rosary turn gold. I experienced strange lights on Cross Mountain late at night despite the lack of electricity there. I marveled at the faith of the many pilgrims as they too experienced these phenomena.

One day we were on the Mountain of Apparitions and everyone saw the "miracle of the sun" except Frank and me. Frank and I just couldn't look into the sun. When we got down to the bottom of the hill, I was finally privileged to see the miracle also. What an experience—to look directly into the sun, experience no discomfort and see all the beautiful things that happen at that moment. Frank was to see it later as he stood alongside St. James Church and experienced the miracle in a very special way.

The little house I stayed in housed five of us—four other men and myself. In five days we became the closest of friends and have remained that way ever since.

My experiences at Medjugorje were innumerable. Just one more—on one of my pilgrimages there was a 74-year-old lady who had a very bad leg. The brace that she wore barely allowed her to walk. She did so with great difficulty. She had suffered with that leg for 20 years. Her many operations were only minimally successful. But she was determined to climb Cross Mountain with us, and I encouraged her to try. If she tired along the way she could either wait for us to return or I would arrange for someone to help her go back.

Cross Mountain has the stations of the cross along the upward climb. It helps to stop at each of the stations and to spend some time in prayer before going to the next level. Even with these periods of relief, the mountain is still very difficult to climb because of its rugged terrain. This good woman started up with us and after a while I forgot about her. I was too busy concentrating on myself making the difficult climb and praying at the various stations. When we finally arrived at the top, where a 16-ton cross stands, I looked around and there she was, literally *running* around on the top of the mountain. In amazement I noticed that her brace was gone and she was walking as normally as anyone of us. She *ran* to me and said she was cured. She walked back down that mountain without any difficulty as if she had been hiking for years. Miracle? Who knows? But it certainly helped her faith and mine.

Yes, my whole life as a priest has changed since I have been to Medjugorje. My spiritual life has deepened dramatically. I have always had a great devotion to Our Lady, but that has increased a hundredfold.

This is Mary's time and she is calling all of us back to Christ, her Son. I only wish that every priest and every lay person could experience the faith, love, devotion and mercy of a Medjugorje pilgrimage. I can't wait to get back!

* * *

GRACE TOOK OVER

Fr. Stephen Valenta, O.F.M.—Seaside Park, New Jersey

I first heard of Medjugorje back in 1982. It took four years for me to respond with enough interest to make a pilgrimage there. Even this was not by my own initiative. I was asked by a friend to put a group together and to be its spiritual assistant. This I did. It was the beginning of a new and refreshing love affair with Medjugorje and, through it, with Mary.

Being allowed to share in the devotion to Mary that was enjoyed by my parents, especially that of my mother, I grew up knowing all about Lourdes and Fatima. It was one of the greatest joys of my life when I was able to "repay" my mother for her gift of this devotion by including her in a pilgrimage group going to Lourdes many years before the apparitions began at Medjugorje.

My first encounter with Medjugorje produced no visible effects in me. I rejoiced with the members of my group whose rosaries had turned and who saw the sun pulsate and who were deeply touched by their exposure to the surroundings and the visionaries. I was happy that I went. Within my spirit there was a small conviction that it was all authentic, but it made no direct impact on me.

The following year it was I who initiated a second pilgrimage. This one turned out to be a source of grace for me. I had had various spiritual problems—problems like pride, anxiety, restlessness, looking for depth of spirit and true peace. These were all pretty well resolved because I had promised myself that this second time would be different. I chose not to look for the external signs. I chose, instead, to stay longer in church, to stay away from the crowds and to get a closer look at what Our Lady was saying. It worked! I returned home refreshed, at peace and much more in love with Mary than ever before.

Medjugorje hosted me four more times, twice as a spiritual assistant to groups and twice for my own spiritual growth. There were many sacrifices, especially in the winter, but the dividend was high. Within the period of three years, I was able to pass from a devotion to Mary to a loving personal relationship with her as my caring, heavenly Mother. I will be ever grateful to my friend who coaxed me to go there for the first time. After that, grace took over.

Without a doubt, had it not been for the war, I would have returned another once or twice. I have caught the urgency in Our Lady's more recent messages, also a motherly sadness over the failure of so many to respond to her maternal concern. Touched by a genuine sadness for her, I was moved to get more serious about giving her assistance and became involved with several video cassettes regarding her messages. I also formed the "Heart to Heart Center" in New Jersey. I am presently engaged in the Franciscan Preaching Apostolate.

As a result of my "tacking" on to Our Lady of Medjugorje, the thrust of my parish retreats, days of recollection, and workshops, I have a greater orientation toward the implementation of her messages.

* * *

ENGLISH PILGRIM BISHOP

Bishop Thomas McMahon—Brentwood, England

The sincerity about everyone and everything struck me particularly, not least in the visionaries. On two occasions I attended the apparitions (now held in the choir loft). And I had a lengthy chat with Marija in her home. As for the general doctrine and messages coming to us from Our Lady via the visionaries, they all square perfectly with Church teaching and have deep Scriptural roots.

I also speak admiringly of the Franciscan staff and their wonderful zeal and patience in coping with the pilgrim multitudes. These throng the place day and night. And in the jam-packed church, where there's hardly even standing room and the summer heat is oppressive, they display deep devotion during those rather lengthy liturgies.

The "Eucharistic dimension" is another thing that is impressive. It indicates that Our Lady is here directing us toward her Son—as she always does. The counsel she gave at Cana virtually encapsulates everything Medjugorje teaches us.

Those who go are hungry and thirsty for the things of the Spirit, and somehow, there in Medjugorje, they find an answer. (From *The Medjugorje Messenger*.)

SPIRITUAL BENEFITS

Archbishop Philip M. Hannan, President, WLAE TV 32
New Orleans, Louisiana

The conversions made by pilgrims to Medjugorje, especially among the youth, have been impressive. These pilgrimages have resulted in people receiving the Sacrament of Reconciliation, receiving Holy Communion, faithful attendance at Mass on Sundays, as well as frequent attendance at Mass on weekdays, recitation of the Rosary and occasional fasting.

The Scriptural counsel of Christ, "by their fruits you shall know them," allows us to judge that the influence at Medjugorje comes from the grace of God. The fruits are undeniably good. Furthermore, the good fruits have been seen in many pilgrims who universally attest that the trip to Medjugorje produced these fruits.

I am also influenced by the fact that the fruits have endured. Many of the pilgrims have maintained these pious practices over a period of years, and their constancy has been a source of inspiration and conversion of others.

It is also notable that no pressure is applied by any of the priests or visionaries at Medjugorje upon the pilgrims to participate in the practice of their faith. There is no "program" at Medjugorje. I specifically inquired of one of the priests in St. James Parish if there was an effort on their part to encourage the pilgrims to ascend Apparition Hill or Mt. Krizevac or to attend Mass, and he replied very firmly in the negative. This means that the religious practices performed by the pilgrims are the result of their initiative.

I found that the physical "marvels," such as the rotation of the sun and the gilding of rosaries, were not major factors in the conversion of the pilgrims I met.

Additionally, the pilgrims are willing to accept a definitive judgment by the Holy See regarding the authenticity of the apparitions seen by the visionaries.

In view of the above facts, I have thought that pilgrimages to Medjugorje can be sources of spiritual benefits to pilgrims. Therefore I encouraged them.

FROM ENGLAND

Fr. George Tutto—London, England

My first visit to Medjugorje was in May 1984. I was drawn there not so much by the reported daily apparitions of Our Lady to six teenagers since June 24, 1981, but rather by what I had heard about the wonderful transformation in the lives of the people of Medjugorje and of its district in response to our Blessed Lady's visitation. The fact that Medjugorje, comprising five hamlets, Medjugorje proper, Bijakovići, Miletina, Vionica, and Šurmanci, near Mostar, the capital of Hercegovina in Yugoslavia, is in a (then) Communist country, added a strong motivation to my visit: if such things could happen in a Communist country, I must see it for myself.

Deeply moved by what I experienced during my first visit to Medjugorje, I made a promise to Our Lady. On the last evening when I was privileged once again to be with the visionaries in the chapel during the apparition of Our Lady, I placed on the altar a letter in which I vowed to make her messages of peace known to others, and I also promised—inspired by the people of Medjugorje, young and old—to devote the rest of my life to promoting the cause of peace, Christ's peace, in response to the invitation of Mary, the Queen of Peace.

In the course of the past few years my conviction has increased even more, thanks to the grace of the Holy Spirit conveyed through the simple but powerful message of our Blessed Lady.

As far as I am concerned, in my weakness and wretchedness, I need all the help the merciful God can give me and I believe that the Mother of Mercy is sent by God in our time to help me and all my brothers and sisters to live the Gospel of her Son Jesus to the full. All this means a moral obligation for me to follow the injunction of St. Paul.

Do not stifle the Spirit or despise the gift of prophecy with contempt; test everything and hold on to what is good and shun every form of evil. (1 Thessalonians 5:19-22.)

(From *"Living the Gospel With Our Lady,"* Manchester Medjugorje Center.)

FAITH, GOODNESS, JOY

Rev. Msgr. Richard T. Nugent—Orchard Park, New York

When I first learned about Medjugorje from a local Croatian priest, Fr. Chris Coric, I was amazed that the Mother of God had been appearing daily since June 24, 1981. But the more I thought about it, the more I felt it was a necessary action from Heaven, given the normal slow reaction and acceptance by the ordinary person to such messages. Even now, after eleven years of daily apparitions, there continues an air of indifference and incredulity on the part of our Catholic bishops, priests and people.

It is true that the official teaching Church has yet to pronounce on this phenomena in Medjugorje, yet millions have attested to something of special interest happening there by their presence and faith.

On my first visit in October 1987, and continuing through three additional visits to the present day, the faith and prayer life of both the villagers and countless visitors are obvious. The many conversions, confessions, communions and individual spiritual healings attest to the "good tree" producing good fruit, as given in the Gospel. The genuine goodness and joy of the visionaries, coupled with their external simplicity and patience, was an example to all who came to Medjugorje.

It is a difficult and trying trip to this mountainous village, and still more trying to climb the hills and mountains. Yet no one seems too tired or unwilling to make the climbs.

The Franciscan Fathers and Religious Sisters remain at service without any expectancy of reward. Even if it will not be accepted some day by the official Church, Medjugorje will have meant an experience worth undertaking. People from all over the world take home with them an experience that continues to enrich their spiritual lives.

Although some in Medjugorje look for special signs of Mary's presence and God's influence on the village, the main evident sign continues to be the faith of the villagers and visitors. It is difficult to visit Medjugorje without receiving an increase in your spiritual life.

3 Cs!

Fr. Bartholomew O'Brien—Horseheads, New York

To me, Medjugorje means: C and C and C. The three Cs! Let me explain.

My visit to Medjugorje was in August of 1988. For some strange reason (maybe it was inspired!) my first reaction to the thrill of being present in this blessed area was to ask not to witness a miracle.

This request of mine was directed to Jesus. It was not the result of meditation. Nor was it the result of prayers offered for special intentions in preparation for the visit. It came to me suddenly, without consultation or prolonged thought. The request was:

"Dear Lord, do not let me see a miracle!" Jesus heard my request. No miracle came my way. In fact, no thought of a miracle came my way...until days later, at the end of my pilgrimage. Then this thought rushed into my mind:

"What about the sun! No one has reminded me to look at the sun. No one seems to be looking up at the sun." Different books tell us that the sun at times spins in the sky and emits beautiful colors.

This thought to look at the sun rushed into my mind but the same thought rushed out—and nothing happened. No miracle, except my very own miracle of having no miracle.

In Medjugorje, Jesus is talking to us. Today, His messages come to us in various ways, especially through His Mother, Mary.

What are these *messages* of Jesus to us, His children, being sent through His beloved Mother, Mary? Personally, they are for me just three. The messages are many, but for practical and realistic reasons, these can be reduced to three.

The three are:

1. *Conversion:* The word means *to change;* that is, to acquire different attitudes and beliefs. Catholics particularly are called to convert, to change their lifestyle, to give witness to the way of life exemplified by Jesus and the saints and taught by Holy Mother Church.

2. *Confession:* Certainly we can list the Sacrament of Penance, Confession, as one of the greatest gifts God has ever given to His people. The power of confession forgives sins and strengthens against future sins. It purifies the soul and heals the wounds of sin. That is why Satan is determined to destroy confession.

Through His Mother, Jesus said: *One must invite the Christians to confession every month, especially the first Saturday of the month.* (The Transfiguration, 1982.)

Again through Mary, Jesus spoke: *Do not confess through sheer habit, in order to remain the same after it. Confession ought to give new life to your faith.* (Nov. 7, 1983.)

3. *Creed:* The Creed, commonly known as The Apostles' Creed, is powerful. Creeds go before deeds. As you think, you'll act. That is why Our Lady insists on the praying of the Creed. She insists also because the Creed has been having but little influence on our Catholic population. Few children know how to pray the Creed. Many adults have forgotten the Creed. For others, the Creed is only a prayer one says to begin the Rosary.

On February 10, 1982, Vicka said, "Our Lady's favorite prayer is the Creed. When we recite it, Our Lady does not cease to smile. I think that no one has ever seen her happier than during this prayer."

So for me, Medjugorje means:

C — CONVERSION!
C — CONFESSION!
C — CREED!

For me, Medjugorje is not a place to witness miracles. For me, Medjugorje is a place to hear MESSAGES. For me, Medjugorje is JESUS SPEAKING to us through His Mother.

A LIGHT TO THE NATIONS

The Monk Joseph—Redwood Valley, California

I must admit that I have never managed to get to Medjugorje myself, although I have followed the events and messages closely since 1983. I've tried to go three times, but the trip had to be cancelled each time. Perhaps the Lord is telling me that monks should stay in their monasteries! At any rate, I hope this doesn't disqualify me as a "witness." (I also witness to Christ's Resurrection, but I have never seen Him!)

When Simeon took the infant Jesus from the arms of Mary in the Temple, he said that He would be *a light of revelation to the nations* (*Lk.* 2:32). The Church has been living more or less perfectly in His Light ever since. It is clear to Catholics (and all Christians of good will and sound theology) that Our Lady *walks in the light as He is in the light* (*1 Jn.* 1:7) in a way that surpasses all other creatures. It is she, the Woman clothed with the sun, whom the Lord has sent to Medjugorje to reflect His Light in a special way, to shine upon and attract a world living in darkness.

Medjugorje is situated in a crossroads of cultures and religions. It has become, over the years, accessible to people of all nations, and the various media have brought the message of Medjugorje to many who could not go there personally. To this obscure village, the Mother of God has come for nothing less than the conversion of the whole world. *I will make you a light to the nations,* says the Lord, *that my salvation may reach to the ends of the earth* (*Is.* 49:6).

When "the nations" are spoken of in the Old Testament, that usually referred to the Gentiles, i.e., all those not belonging to the Chosen People. Now, after Christ, St. Paul calls those who believe in Jesus the true children of Abraham. But "the nations" still surround the Church; the world is still full of unbelievers who have not seen the light. Mirjana has received a special task from Our Lady to pray for these, and it is for the sake of the conversion of the multitudes that Our Lady urges our own deeper conversion and commitment to prayer and fasting.

The Lady of all nations has attracted Orthodox, Protestants, Jews, Moslems, Buddhists and others to her shrine. Yet Medjugorje is in no way a center of a false ecumenism that compromises Gospel and Tradition. The message of unity is based on forgiveness, love, and mutual respect, rather than on blurring distinctions at the expense of doctrine. Therefore, a deep Catholic piety is practiced and preached in Medjugorje. The truth and power of the Faith are its own witnesses.

The Queen of Peace here expresses one of her Heart's desires: *I wish that you all be the reflection of Jesus, which will enlighten this unfaithful world walking in darkness. I wish all of you to be the light for everyone and that you give witness in the light* (June 5, 1986). Thus our Blessed Mother commissions each of those who have received grace through Medjugorje to be a light for others, and not a lamp hiding under a bushel basket (*Matt.* 5:15-16).

We have been warned repeatedly by the Virgin Mary to be aware of Satan's tactics and to be strong against him. So it should not be surprising that there are those who hate the light and prefer darkness. Medjugorje has suffered severely from such, but the message has still gone out, and countless souls have been renewed in their love for Jesus and Mary (or have embraced them for the first time). *The light shines on in darkness, and the darkness has not overcome it* (*Jn.* 1:5).

We do not know what the future will bring, but we can be sure that Medjugorje, each of us, and the whole world are in the hands of God and the hands of Mary. Ours is not to speculate but to pray and live the messages, to consecrate ourselves to Our Mother's Heart, and allow her to lead us ever more deeply into the Heart of Jesus, the Light of the world.

GOD'S WORK IN MY WEAKNESS

Fr. Al Winshman, S.J.—Boston, Massachusetts

With the coming of the Virgin Mary, our Mother and Queen of Peace, to all of us at Medjugorje since June 24, 1981, I have experienced many graces of conversion as a Catholic priest. I have been delighted and amazed at the things that have happened in my life which I am able to understand as coming from Jesus through Mary. Before, I was simply doing *my* thing for God, and since then I am slowly experiencing that God is doing *His* thing in and through me. What a difference this growing surrender to God makes as it brings His strength and peace into my weakness.

The growing desire I had for many years for a retreat ministry at a Jesuit retreat house became a reality in the summer of 1981 with my assignment to Loyola Retreat House in Faulkner, Maryland. There I received an unexpected grace. I was gifted to have superiors who truly respected the movements of the Spirit within me and nurtured my own response in freedom. Mary came into my life in a new and powerful way, although I would not hear about Medjugorje until the fall of 1984. But my story really blossomed from seeds planted and germinated years before.

When my mother was a young girl her family was converted and baptized together because my grandparents hungered for daily Mass and Holy Communion. They also had a tremendous devotion to Mary, and they prayed the daily family Rosary. My father came into the Catholic Church when he married my mother. And so, as the eldest child, born in 1934, I grew up in a family of faith, praying daily the family Rosary and joining my mother as a youngster for morning Mass. I was only seven years old when, as we left St. Mary's Church in Dedham, Massachusetts, one morning, I told her that I was going to become a priest. That desire never left me and now intensifies. Mary brings us to Jesus.

On St. Ignatius' feastday in 1952, I entered the Jesuit novitiate right out of high school and on my first anniversary as a Jesuit consecrated myself, my life and future priesthood, to Jesus through the hands of Mary in the DeMontfort total consecration and surrender of my life. My personal motto became "To Jesus through Mary." However, as I now look back, my earlier spiritual progress was jeopardized and eroded by our modern world culture in its materialistic atheism, sensuality and individualism that began taking an increasing toll during and after the late sixties. But in the summer of 1981, my spiritual life once again grew when I consciously began saying my "Yes!" to the challenging yet gentle call heard within my heart.

Our Lady was to be the one who would call me back and mold me anew as a Catholic and a priest. I was never so happy as I was at the retreat house. A new spirit energized me. By the summer of 1984 I was again praying the Rosary which had lain dormant in my pocket for years. Later that fall I took seriously conversion and its basic starting point, to consciously turn away from the occasions of sin. I became deeply troubled by the insensitivity to sin in our lives. Sadly, annual retreatants were not going to confession. They said they had nothing to confess, even though they admitted living the lifestyles of the TV "soap operas," saying, "But Father, today that's no longer sinful." I realized that the mass media, with its strong anti-Gospel message, was responsible for much of the present day sin and hardness of heart. As with movies, I now put the habitual and indiscriminate use of TV out of my life. Wow, I was beginning to live Mary's call to prayer and fasting and I hadn't heard of Medjugorje yet.

As I become more reflective, I see how Mary was guiding me back to a faithful unity with the teachings of the Church, clearly proclaimed by Pope John Paul II today in a world that refuses to listen. Some of my thinking during the seventies had imperceptibly become tainted with the erroneous new theology, as I rationalized ways to justify this and that, for myself and for others. For this I have since repented and ask forgiveness from all whom I may have led astray into what were euphemistically called "gray" areas. I believe that deep within our hearts we know what is right and wrong and what we need to do. I am realizing more the absolute priority prayer must have in my life so that I can come to listen deeply in quiet stillness and inner reflection to God revealing Himself and speaking to me. That is what Mary is now teaching the world today in her school of "prayer of the heart" at Medjugorje.

It was in the late fall of 1984 that I first heard of Mary's daily apparitions in Medjugorje. I was initially angry that word of this had been kept quiet in the Church, so that I was just hearing of it more than three years later. That winter I read everything

I could get my hands on. Stan Karminski and his family had gone there several times and made a documentary video, "A Message of Peace." In March 1985 I visited them and got a copy of their video. With this my ministry began to take a whole new direction as I showed the video and spoke on the events of Medjugorje everywhere I went. Fr. Joseph Pelletier's book, "The Queen of Peace Visits Medjugorje," which Stan helped to document, gave me a clear presentation of the events and the message.

By the end of that summer I had an inner conviction that I had to go to Medjugorje. This, as I've learned, is a grace that Mary gives to those whom she calls. But how was I to go to Medjugorje? In discernment I revealed this to my superior, Fr. Clem Petrik, S.J., at the retreat house. His unexpected response was another grace from Mary. He knew that since I had been incorporating Mary's message and call at Medjugorje in my retreats, many graces of conversion had come to retreatants, and so he commissioned me to go and investigate Medjugorje. In November 1985 I went as a pilgrim while it was still a poor village with no heat in the homes except the kitchen stove. The simple pastoral setting was not yet spoiled by extensive construction undertaken to cope with the millions of pilgrims.

On that, my first pilgrimage, we were housed in homes in the neighboring village of Citluk and arrived at the church at 6:30 p.m., in the middle of the evening Croatian Mass. The church was overflowing with hundreds outside and 1600 or more inside. The faith and prayer of the people immediately told me that this was real. In the next few days I met the visionaries and began entering into the life of the village. The following summer I began leading spiritual pilgrimages to Medjugorje and have taken over twenty pilgrim groups there by the fall of 1991. Today Medjugorje is a second home and its people are like family to me.

Back at the retreat house I was getting more and more calls to go out to parishes to give Medjugorje Evenings of Prayer. Mary asks us above all to pray—to pray and live the Rosary and the Mass. My three-hour evenings of prayer, faithful to Medjugorje, begin with the meditated Rosary before sharing on the apparitions and messages of Mary, and conclude with the Holy Sacrifice of the Mass and a healing blessing. By 1988 I had to discern whether to cut back on my ministry and continue on staff at the retreat house, or be assigned full-time to my growing Marian ministry.

Mary again called me. Contrary to all expectations, my Provincial Superior called me back to Boston, formally assigning me full-time to my Marian Renewal Ministry. This ministry has taken me from England to Mexico, from Alaska to the Caribbean, and throughout the U.S. and Canada, giving Marian Evenings, retreats and parish missions, and speaking at conferences.

For me personally, the grace of striving to live more fully our Mother's call at Medjugorje, which is the Fatima call—lively faith, prayer and fasting, conversion, frequent confession and living the Mass—has brought me to a growing devotion to the Holy Eucharist, Mary and the Church. This brings an inner peace to the extent that I am true to God, my neighbor and myself. I would not want to return to my life as it was before our Mother and Queen of Peace began coming to our world at Medjugorje. Praised be Jesus and Mary now and forever!

* * *

MARY, OUR COSMIC MOTHER

Fr. Francis J. Babbish, S.J.

Of the more recent apparitions of Mary, Medjugorje is undoubtedly the most extraordinary of all—eleven years of continuous apparitions and messages to the millions of pilgrims and to the people all over the world. Most people derive a sense of urgency from this reported phenomenon.

Making a review of the main message in each of the major apparitions, there is a progression of teaching and exhortation from Mary to lead us to her Son and our accepting of Him as our personal Savior and Lord, and the frame of mind and condition of soul that help toward that end. The underlying message is that Mary does not want herself to be the center of attention, but her one and only purpose is to lead us to her Son. As she told Gabriel, she wants to be known as the *"Handmaid of the Lord."* At Lourdes, Fatima and Medjugorje, she spells out the details of how to proceed, and always polite as she is, she will say, *Thank you for responding to my call.* (Fr. Babbish passed away in January, 1990.)

NEW CHRISTMAS

Fr. Jim Duffy—Canada

If Jesus, Mary and Joseph obeyed the Father's will by living in Nazareth for 30 years, it could only be because God had a great and important lesson to teach us. If Mary, the Mother of God, has been appearing to the 'children' of Medjugorje, since the 24th of June, 1981, on a daily basis, then the Lord must also have something important and profound to teach us. I respectfully await the Church's finding about the authenticity of these private revelations, but in the meantime I feel obliged to share with you very briefly, my own personal experience.

The best words I have heard to date that describe what is happening is a "New Christmas." Once again Mary has come to give us her Son, and He in turn utters the words of the Gospel: *Repent, for the Kingdom of God is at hand.* What I believe I saw and felt and touched, was a renewed people...a renewed Christian parish, simply because they have heard the Word of God and responded to it. What are the signs of a renewed People of God? Obviously, the same as the Gospel—first of all, serious sin has practically been eliminated in and around the community of Medjugorje, according to the Pastor...(from *"Medjugorje Reflections"* Koinonia Publishers.)

* * *

Murilo S. Krieger, Bishop of Florianopolis, Brazil

"The Pope told me:
—Medjugorje is a great center of spirituality.

He spoke to me in Portuguese" (letter of February 24 1990, in *Eco*, November 1990).

A LINGERING MEMORY

Fr. Joseph Fertal, S.V.D.—Los Angeles, California

It has been a year since I was privileged to make a pilgrimage to Medjugorje. The euphoria of the experience has not yet worn off.

I did not go to Medjugorje out of curiosity or to resolve any lingering doubts. Ever since reading about the apparitions years earlier, I felt convinced and attracted to the place, never realizing that an opportunity—a free gift—would be available to actually be present in person. The offer came a few days before Christmas (1990) and it was the best Christmas gift I received. Then too, the pleasure of the gift was further enhanced since the plane trip began on March 19th, my feastday, and the first day of the activities started on my 60th birthday. (What more pleasant surprises can an individual hope for?) I went to Medjugorje primarily to be present at a place where I believed Mary was appearing then and now. I wanted to stand on the very ground blessed by her special presence, and hopefully meet at least some of the individuals privileged to hear and see the Blessed Virgin. How fortunate and honored they were! Without reading over past impressions put into writing shortly after the trip, certain memories still stay in my mind.

The penitential aspect of the place impressed me the most and continues to do so even today. Books and several videotapes did not convey the rugged steepness of the winding paths and the sharp, jagged rocks that needed to be struggled over on the way up Mt. Podbrdo and Mt. Krizevac. (Of course, with my hip transplant, I did not dare to go for the several evening visits planned by the seers at the place of the apparitions.)

The spirit of prayer and peace that pervaded the atmosphere and prevailed over the huge crowds during the late afternoon rosaries, prayed simultaneously in several languages in St. James Church, still stand out very strongly in my memory.

Thirdly, the interviews and sharings given by the visionaries, especially by Ivanka Ivankovic Elez (in whose home I had the privilege to board and be waited upon by her for seven full days), by Vicka Ivankovic (who encouraged me to stay at her place since I got accidentally(?) left behind by the rest of my group), and by Ivan Dragicevic who filled us in with many personal details and fine points not found in the books. Their humility, simplicity and sincerity still stands out in my mind.

As a result of my visit to Medjugorje I feel that my devotion to Mary has been strengthened and improved. My praying the Rosary has increased from five decades to all fifteen. I preach about Mary at every opportunity possible and make frequent references to the pilgrimage. Unfortunately, at the age of 60 plus, I find the fasting aspect a little difficult to fulfill (I think I am "addicted" to caffeine).

I pray daily that peace will soon come again to Yugoslavia so that the pilgrimages can resume and people may return to God or come closer to Him as a result of Mary's apparitions which I presume are still continuing even though the crowds are not there. Some day—God willing—I will get a chance to return, perhaps as a chaplain to some group or even organizing one myself. The first trip was somewhat hectic, and it whizzed by too quickly. Hopefully, the second time around will be different—less rushing to see and hear everything and more praying and reflecting on Podbrdo and Mt. Krizevac, and being more selective in my activities.

Even if the "special sign or miracle" does not occur and the Church eventually allows the happenings at Medjugorje to phase itself out, still I feel it has done a tremendous good for the millions who have gone to Medjugorje. In most cases, it was their faith, love and devotion to Mary that brought them there, and I'm convinced they left the place all the better for being present. They returned home more devout and prayerful (maybe even more resigned to their sickness or unavoidable problem). I feel this is the reason why the Vatican is somewhat reluctant to pass judgment on the validity of the daily apparitions—because of the tremendous spiritual benefits possible and resulting for those who go there believing. Even if a decision is made that the visions are not able to be proved beyond doubt, still, for me it was a beautiful experience, a real spiritual shot in the arm.

Medjugorje is now a memory that continues to linger in my mind, a memory, thank God, that will not go away. I hope and pray that many others will also some day have the privilege to make such a pilgrimage and be moved by the experience, by the encouraging visits of Mary in our own day and age.

WHAT IS MEDJUGORJE?

Msgr. Leo A. Hoffmann—Ft. Wayne, Indiana

What is Medjugorje? In four words, Medjugorje is: "To Jesus through Mary." In God's eternal plan of redemption, Mary was chosen from all women to enflesh the eternal Son so He could be one of us in all things save sin.

From the moment Mary answered *"Fiat"*—let it be done according to your word—until the day she stood beneath the Cross and heard the words of her dying Son, *Woman, behold your son,* and then to John, *Behold your mother,* she was Jesus' mother only. However, from that moment on she became mother of all mankind. While remaining the mother of Jesus, she is my mother and your mother.

From time to time, Jesus sends His mother on mission to His younger brothers and sisters, His mother's other children, to call us to conversion, penance, prayer, to reform us into true children of God. To help accomplish this mission, Mary chooses little people by worldly standards. Witness Guadalupe, LaSalette, Lourdes, Fatima, Banneaux (Belgium) and now Medjugorje.

For eleven years, Mary has been revealing her Son's call to us. It has been my privilege to make five pilgrimages to Medjugorje. From time to time, people ask why I go to Medjugorje so often. My response: Medjugorje is home to me. Home is where your mother is, and Mary is my mother. My heavenly mother has been visiting us in this previously unknown village for eleven years through Maria, Vicka, Jakov, Ivan, Ivanka and Mirjana. I have never seen Mary face to face, nor have I heard her voice, but I have been present in the room when she spoke to a visionary. Believe me when I say I felt her presence. I knew my Mother was in the room. Immediately after the vision, a translator gave us the message in English (all present, some 106 clergy were English speaking). Her message was a special call to priests.

Occasionally, a complaint is heard. Why does the Blessed Mother repeat the same message over and over. In answer: remember she is Mother and we are children. As mothers do, Mary finds it necessary to repeat over and over the same message until we grasp and act on it. And sometimes, she has to reprimand us.

Recently, she told us: *You are praying a little and you are doing a little penance, but you must do much more before peace comes.*

Mary's mission is to lead us to her Divine Son. The center of Medjugorje is St. James Church, where pilgrims from all over the world congregate in great numbers hour after hour to celebrate Eucharist in their native languages, and receive the sacraments and instruction. Speaking of sacraments, I must tell you that I have spent many hours in a confessional at St. James center reconciling sinners to God.

A pilgrimage to Medjugorje is just the beginning. Once people make a pilgrimage they remain devout children of Mary for life. They return home to participate in Eucharist daily or as often as their lives permit, pray the Rosary, fast and do other penances. Thousands renew themselves by making Medjugorje conferences at Notre Dame, New Orleans, Rosemont, Dallas and Oregon.

Years ago, I listened to Archbishop Fulton J. Sheen as he said, "Mary is treacherous. She will betray you into the hands of her Divine Son."

* * *

Father Paola Giurati

Father Paola Giurati, a sociologist, raised in the United States, and professor at the major seminary in Padua, has proven his credibility through studies at this sanctuary and at Our Lady of Lourdes. He also studied Medjugorje and published his first results in the Italian review *Jesus.*

Fr. Giurati states: "People go to Medjugorje for essentially religious reasons. They are happy to have an existential experience there without separation. They find there a reassessment. They are committed as at Lourdes, and perhaps more so; and one finds in Medjugorje a synchronization and a homogenety between the message which the pilgrims receive and that which they express. All that shows a good operation of social communication." (Taken from *Eight Years,* The Riehle Foundation.)

WHY ARE ROSARIES CHANGING COLOR?

Fr. John Szantyr—Worcester, Massachusetts

In early spring of 1987, I heard news about rosaries turning the color of gold. Having recollection of similar claims made at a questionable scene of apparitions in America, I became concerned that the Medjugorje prodigy could be diabolically inspired. I was afraid that pilgrims were being distracted from the message and purpose of Our Lady's visitations. Having planned a 30 day retreat in Medjugorje in August, 1987, I intended to crusade against this danger.

Not long after my arrival in Medjugorje I observed that people were accepting these events quietly, faithfully and as a sign of God's love and presence there. I began to consider the prodigy from a different point of view. I turned to prayer seeking light from the Holy Spirit. If this is from God, I thought, there should be a message attached.

During my prayer, these words came to me: *"As in the furnace he proved them."* I searched Scripture for these words and found them in *Wisdom* 3:5-6. *Chastised a little, they shall be greatly blessed because God tried them and found them worthy of Himself. As gold in the furnace he proved them.* I received my answer! With reflection and inspiration from the Holy Spirit I adapted this teaching to the phenomenon of "golden rosaries."

When gold ore is mined it comes from the earth unrefined and impure. The gold must be separated from the foreign elements clinging to it. In order to do this, the gold ore must pass through a hot furnace where the impurities are burned away, leaving in the end pure gold. The scriptural text from the book *Wisdom* likens us to gold. The human soul, that golden nugget which has been mined from the earth of sinfulness through the loving act of Christ's Redemption, brought to salvation through the merciful love of the Divine Gold Miner (God the Father), needs to enter a purifying transformation.

How does a soul arrive at this kind of purification? Conversion is the beginning of the refining process of that gold nugget we call "soul." We enter into purification as we decide to enter into a conversion of life, to turn away from sin and anything related to sin. The rosary we carry is a symbol of ourselves—a living rosary.

The cross on the rosary symbolizes our faith and our willingness to suffer with Christ by carrying our daily crosses. Through abandonment we let God purify us through the furnace of fire represented in our daily problems, illnesses, aggravations, anxieties, fears, pains, cares, etc. Each link on the rosary, connected to each other and finally to the bead, represents the suffering and crosses of our daily lives. Since these links alone turn gold on a chosen rosary, God is giving the possessor a message to begin to live the message of conversion.

We have to actively accept this process of being cleaned. If we accept conversion we will be purified by the gentle fire of His holy love in and through the Holy Spirit.

In summary, what is this prodigy telling us? A change taking place on our rosaries is a call to personal conversion, to personal purification of our souls by the acceptance of each trial in our daily lives which represent that "furnace of fire" making us holy. If God has blessed any one of us with this sign, His purpose is not to initiate boasting, entertainment or hysterical wonder. It is simply a personal message given to each of us to respond to His call to be holy.

P.S. My rosaries turned a gold color recently. I suddenly found myself entering a new period of unexpected trials. I am reminded that my purification is for my greater holiness. My deeper prayer life will sustain me to the end. (From an article, *Medjugorje Magazine*.)

FAITH AND PRAYER

Fr. Francis Budovic, S.J.—Chicago, Illinois

If I may be spontaneous in expressing my thoughts about what Medjugorje means to me, then it would be concisely: "The same that faith and prayer mean to me." I cannot live fully or abundantly without them. They contribute much to the preserving and growth of my spiritual life and spiritual wisdom. Faith and prayer are the eagle's wings on which God carries the soul over the deserts and wastelands of this earthly existence, and Medjugorje's pedagogy had an impact on both my life of faith and my life of prayer. Medjugorje, as a center of faith and prayer, has offered me an insight so helpful for renewing my inner vision of God, of the Blessed Mother, of myself, of other people, of life and of the world. And my renewed vision has influenced a good deal of my personality, at least that is my feeling, and also an observation of my co-pilgrims who still speak about certain changes in me.

When I was in the fourth grade, just before I had become an altar boy, I had an extraordinary experience of God's love, of peace and joy as I was praying in the church during Holy Mass. I remember it well. As I was sitting on my heels behind the baptismal font, located close to the altar, I felt Jesus' presence. Although I was not able to think great deep or high thoughts about God or God's marvelous works, I perceived deep peace and joy, and I had no will, no desire to leave my good praying spot, although all the worshipers who attended the Holy Mass left the church in a hurry, especially the children. I believe now, it was a case of what Saint Ignatius of Loyola describes in his Spiritual Exercises:

> "God alone can give consolation to the soul without any previous cause. It belongs solely to the Creator to come into a soul, to leave it, to act upon it, to draw it wholly to the love of His Divine Majesty. I said without previous cause, that is, without any preceding perception or knowledge of any subject by which a soul might be led to such a consolation through its own acts of intellect and will."

I believe now, that this prayer-experience was the first grace of my religious vocation. My heart desired to have more experiences of such spiritual joy and peace, and so I started to develop a habit of making visits to Jesus in the Blessed Sacrament and began to consider entering the Society of Jesus. One day, after returning home from school, I entered the church to pray and there was my mother, alone, praying in the pew. I went to her and whispered in her ear: "Mother, I'm thinking of becoming a Jesuit." She said, "I am praying for you, you pray more and make a good decision."

My Medjugorje experience is a renewal of that prayer spot behind the baptismal font, combined with my visits to Jesus, and that mother in the pew is now my Blessed Mother. I am whispering into her ear my heart's desires and she reassures me; she is praying, interceding for me and asking me to pray with her: *Pray, pray, pray from the heart.*

My devotion to the Blessed Mother has changed significantly. I do not feel good if I don't pray the whole Rosary, fifteen decades daily. Immediately after returning from my first pilgrimage to Medjugorje, I started my own prayer group, which meets every Friday, and I look forward to it with joy. I always prayed the Rosary daily since my mother taught me to pray in my early childhood, and then as a Jesuit novice, I started to pray the Holy Rosary in Latin and I still do when praying privately. The more I feel that the Blessed Mother is also my mother, the more I feel like a child and desire to be, because Jesus said: *I assure you, that whoever does not accept the reign of God like a little child shall not take part in it.* (*Mark* 10:15).

On my first pilgrimage to Medjugorje, I was often asked by my pilgrims if I believe in the apparitions, and I preferred to answer such questions with the words of the Gospel, specifically the words of Saint Thomas the Apostle: *Until I have seen, I cannot believe.* I did not receive any apparition, but I got its equivalent. Talking with the visionaries made me feel like talking with the Blessed Mother. It was convincing because their answers testified to their progress in the school of spiritual life taught them by Mary. I sensed in them the spiritual maturity of simple, sincere, faith and trust in God and the Blessed Mother. I saw their patience as the fruit of their humility.

Medjugorje, for me, is an international place of prayer and of faith and I was very pleased to read what Cardinal Ratzinger, the prefect of the Congregation for the Doctrine of the Faith, has to say on Medjugorje:

"We want to take care that this place which has become a place of prayer and of faith, continues to be, and comes even more to be, perfectly one with the Church." (Medjugorje: Gebetsaktion Maria, #22.)

Medjugorje revived and strengthened my faith and prayer and especially enriched my life with the feeling that the Blessed Mother is also my Mother and we all are her children with the assured inheritance of the Kingdom of Heaven. It also helped me to have a good relationship of deep esteem and respect for my pilgrims and to perceive the beneficial influence of their spirit of faith and prayer.

Like Jesus was amazed when he found faith in the centurion and remarked to His followers, *I assure you, I have never found this much faith in Israel* (*Matt.* 8:10), I, too, was amazed, and admired the faith of my pilgrims. I have never found elsewhere such a faith as in the pilgrims to Medjugorje.

* * *

EMBRACE OF HEAVENLY LOVE

Fr. Don Schmidt—Horicon, Wisconsin

For me, Medjugorje has become part of a spiritual renewal in my life. The experiences of my five pilgrimages to Medjugorje have helped me to know in my heart that we truly have a God Who loves us deeply, Who through His Son, Jesus, continues to save us, reconcile us, that the Hoy Spirit leads and guides us all, and that Mary our Mother cares for all God's children and wants to bring everyone to Him. We are all in an eternal embrace of heavenly love and peace, and that message is being given for all the world to know and to live.

Wherever God acts and works sovereignly in this world, signs and wonders accompany Him. What I have seen, heard, reflected on, prayed over, witnessed in the lives of other pilgrims, experienced in my own spiritual journey with the Lord Jesus, all these confirm for me what I feel is the truth about the phenomenon of Medjugorje.

THE CROSS AND MEDJUGORJE

Fr. Stanley Smolenski—Enfield, Connecticut

The plain of Medjugorje is surrounded by beautiful hills and mountains. That is how it got its name: "Mid Hills," between the mountains. Two mountains now dominate the area: the hill of the cross and the hill of the apparitions.

The hill of the cross, Krizevac, is so called because in the Holy Year of 1933, the 19th centenary of Redemption, the villagers built a forty foot concrete cross on its summit. Only when one sees the treacherously steep, rocky paths these people had to climb to carry all the necessary materials, does one appreciate their sacrificial faith. Our Lady is reported to have said that the providence of God took that cross into account. On the Feast of the Exaltation of the Cross, September 14, vast crowds have gathered each year there for the celebration of Mass.

Mary identified herself to the six young visionaries at Medjugorje as the Queen of Peace. In view of these two presences, it recalls what St. Paul told the Colossians *(Col. 1:20) Christ made peace through the blood of His Cross.*

As the cross is very much a part of the landscape of Medjugorje, so is it also a characteristic of its spirituality. Sacramental life abounds as dozens of priests console repentant sinners with absolution; these same priests then distribute Holy Communion to the overflowing crowds at the Masses. The graces of these sacraments flow from the sacrifice of the Cross.

These farmers, with their simple lifestyle, probably envied the rest of the world, with all of its luxuries. Now, the outside world flies to Medjugorje for that elusive element that the luxurious world cannot give: Peace! From the biblical perspective, that is obviously what St. Paul speaks about in *1 Cor. 1:27*:

God chose those whom the world considers absurd to shame the wise; he singled out the weak of this world to shame the strong. He chose the lowborn and despised, those who count for nothing to reduce to nothing those who are something; so that mankind can do no boasting before God.

Can a practical spirituality be formulated from the events at Medjugorje? That should not be too difficult, since the message revolves around peace. We want permanent peace, not here one day and gone the next. And since Jesus *made peace through the blood of His Cross (Col.* 1:20), the way to peace for us is the same royal way of Jesus—the cross. Since we want daily peace, it must come through our daily cross. Jesus said, *Pick up your cross daily and come follow Me. (Lk.* 9:23). If we learn to live with, then to accept, and finally to love our cross, then we shall develop that peace of Christ.

Today, there are some who stress the elimination of all suffering through healing. But some have a vocation to suffering. And Mary's children are numbered among them. At Fatima, she asked the children if they would accept the suffering God allowed in their lives, for the conversion of sinners. Besides the great moral suffering of misunderstanding and doubt, Jacinta and Francisco were victims of the international influenza epidemic. Jacinta, aged 9, had to undergo an operation, and died alone, separated from family and friends. St. Maximilian Kolbe, the knight of the Immaculata, volunteered to replace a fellow prisoner, offering his life at the death camp at Auschwitz. The list is long.

So, Mary allows a sword to pierce the hearts of some of her children so that they may have perfect spiritual resemblance and identity with her—at the foot of the Cross. Mary helped pay the price of that peace, "made through the blood of His Cross." So, too, if we stand with Mary daily, then she will help us fulfill our duties to God and neighbor through our daily worship and witness, forming the vertical and horizontal beams of our daily cross.

Medjugorje places us mid-hills, between the hill of the Cross and the hill of her presence through the apparitions. She unites us to both, that we may have the effect of both, Peace! As we achieve our personal peace daily, so we can then share that gift with others.

(Part of an article by Fr. Smolenski in QUEEN of all hearts Magazine, Nov.-Dec. 1987.)

THE REAL SECRET OF MEDJUGORJE

Fr. Jack Wintz, O.F.M.—Cincinnati, Ohio

It did not occur to me until I arrived in Medjugorje that the Feast of the Annunciation would fall during the week of my stay. The date of the feast, March 25, also coincided with one of our Our Lady's public messages. The Annunciation Day message came, as usual, through the visionary Maria, who was in Italy on an extended prayer retreat with others from her prayer group. She received the message during her apparition that day. After the apparition, Maria wrote down the Croatian words and read them over the telephone to Father Slavko in Medjugorje. Father Philip Pavich translated the message into English. The Message of March 25, 1988, reads:

> Dear children! Today also I am inviting you to a complete surrender to God. You, dear children, are not conscious of how God loves you with such a great love. Because of it, He permits me to be with you so I can instruct you and help you find the way of peace. That way, however, you cannot discover if you do not pray. Therefore, dear children, forsake everything and consecrate your time to God and then God will bestow gifts upon you and bless you.
>
> Little children, do not forget that your life is fleeting like the spring flower which today is wondrously beautiful, but tomorrow has vanished. Therefore, pray in such a way that your prayer, your surrender to God, may become like a road sign. That way your witness will not only have value for yourselves, but for all of eternity. Thank you for having responded to my call.

I must confess, that as I read over the above message on March 27, Palm Sunday, I experienced a deep peace and, sinner though I am, a deep sense of God's unconditional love and that of Our Lady.

It was a sunny morning and I was sitting on a rock behind the Church of St. James. In those words, I felt some of the "great love" to which Mary is leading us. The message of "complete surrender" seemed so perfect for the feast of Mary's Annunciation.

To me, at the heart of the Medjugorje message is this: The source of the world's healing is first of all God's burning love. It is a loving God who brings about the world's salvation, and not simply our efforts, important as they are as instruments of God's saving will. Only through surrender to God (prayer) can the branch be in living union with the vine and able to bear fruit. The good news out of Medjugorje is the same as the Good News out of Judea: A saving God is with us and invites us to respond.

Mary's messages always end with the words: *Thank you for having responded to my call.* Her own "complete surrender" to God's overflowing love reminds us that she knows much about "responding." If God's "great love" seeking our response is the secret of Medjugorje—and I believe it is—then the world can only be blessed when it accepts this good news.

*   *   *

BITTERSWEET

Fr. John B. Wang

Having spent several decades in academic life, I thought the time had come for me to retire to a quiet, prayerful life. I was wrong. Medjugorje changed that perspective.

Medjugorje has effected in me a rejuvenation. It has brought me a great deal of fresh energy, new vitality, new direction and focus. I firmly believe in Our Lady's visits and her messages. This belief and conviction moved me to organize prayer groups, promote pilgrimages, attend Marian conferences, give talks and show videos both inside and outside the U.S.

These activities have been bittersweet. On one hand, it is painful to face disbelief, cold indifference, skepticism and even antagonism, especially when they come from one's own confreres. On the other hand, it is a great delight to see the devotion, joy, peace and unity of those who heed Mary's call for repentance, prayer and holiness. I feel I am truly blessed to be part of the army that fights under the banner of the Immaculate Heart of Mary, the Woman clothed with the sun, who will crush the head of the Evil One and bring total victory for her Son, Jesus. I am eagerly and confidently awaiting the arrival of this victorious day.

ACCEPT AND USE THE GIFTS

Fr. Augustine Donegan, T.O.R.—Steubenville, Ohio

At Mass today, we heard a Gospel we have heard many times:

*Ask and you will receive, knock and it will be opened,
seek and you will find.*

But the problem is, we ask but we don't wait to receive. We knock and don't wait for it to be opened. We seek but we don't wait to find. We want God to do our will. We say, "Thy will be done, but God, here's my plan, give it Your blessing." We always want God to fit our time schedule, don't we?

This morning, again, He has said to us, *Ask and you will receive.* He says the one who asks **will** receive. Now this is the word of God. God is not kidding. He is not lying. He says if you ask, you will receive. This is the word of God. And He says to us today, "If you ask Me, you will receive. If you look for Me, you will find Me."

So, now all of us are here on a pilgrimage. What are we going to ask God for? And if, in faith, we ask Him, He said He would give it to us. God will give the gift, **but**, we have to accept it, and we have to use it. So, what two gifts does a pilgrimage to Medjugorje suggest? What are we going to bring home with us from here, from this place of apparitions?

I would suggest that we ask for two gifts: First, that we ask God for the gift of full conversion of life; and second, the gift of prayer. If we ask God, He will give them to us.

Somehow, this spells out for me what Medjugorje is really all about: the gift of full conversion, not playing games with God by going to Church Sunday morning and then forgetting Him the rest of the week. Jesus said, *I've come to give you life,* not to play games.

Full conversion! What is this conversion, this repentance that we talk about all week? It is making a U-turn; because every day we tend to go off the road because of our human weakness, the distractions around us. So the gift of full conversion is the gift of a U-turn in our lives. It is a "gift" because we cannot do it ourselves; we are too weak. We need His Spirit. A converted life is a life of living for Jesus Christ. It is not a head trip by which we know certain dogma. It's living it; living for Jesus Christ.

To be converted to God means we cannot go along with the world in which we are living. Let's face it. We live at a time and in a world that has abandoned Jesus Christ. I'm afraid there are too many Christians who live not **in** the world, but **for** the world, playing games with God.

Therefore, a life of full conversion means that we be different, that we don't go along with the world, but we stand up for Jesus Christ and His Gospel and His Church. It's making a choice for Jesus Christ and not the times in which we're living. That hurts; that's the sacrifice. We don't like to fast. That hurts; that's the sacrifice. *That's Gospel.* That is the first gift—full conversion.

The second gift is the gift of prayer. But whoever receives the gift must accept and use it.

We speak of saying prayers, and many times that is all we do; we "say prayers." Hear Mass! Say the Rosary! We have to go beyond the saying. It's like turning on the tape recorder, let it say the Rosary. Prayer at Medjugorje, Mary says, must be from the heart. It's not so much saying, as communicating with God, the praying of the heart.

Mary tells us that the greatest prayer is the Mass, specifically, the Eucharist. Eucharist is really the last prayer of Jesus Christ, sacramentalized. His sacrifice becomes present, and we offer ourselves, "with Him, through Him, and in Him." It's a prayer of Christ, and our prayer, joined together.

Prayer is a gift. We must accept it and use it. That means we must take the time—not only on Sunday morning. Prayer is food and drink for our souls. We eat every day. We must pray every day. Take the time to be with your God. The gift of prayer will be given if we ask.

Jesus invited Peter to get out of the boat and walk on the water. He didn't lift him out of the boat. Peter had to do it. He received the gift, but he had to do his part.

Let us ask God for the gift of full conversion, making religion our life, not a game. Seek the gift of prayer, for those who learn to pray, those who learn to love, are those who live in peace. That is what Medjugorje does. It makes the word of God so concrete.

It puts flesh on it. This town is so down to earth, where the Mother of God appears.

God says, "Ask me, I will give them to you. Will you accept them, and will you use them?" If we do, our lives will change. If you go home the same as you came, then you missed the word that Medjugorje brings. Through Mary's intercession, let the Lord change us. Use the gifts. (Homily at the English Mass, in Medjugorje, Feb. 25, 1988.)

* * *

MOST OF ALL—THE MASS!

Fr. Augustine Davis, O.S.B.—South Pittsburg, Tennessee

I am a Benedictine monk from St. Meinrad Archabbey and currently pastor of Our Lady of Lourdes parish. About four years ago I was invited to go to Medjugorje on a pilgrimage but declined since I didn't know much about it. Then about a year and a half ago I was invited again and accepted with enthusiasm, having done some homework.

The pilgrimage was the beginning of December so as to include the feast of the Immaculate Conception. It was cold there, the housing was poor, the meals were only fair, the church was crowded. Yet, it was a most wonderful spiritual experience. I was very impressed with the confessions I heard, up to two and one half hours each day. Miracles of grace happened through them. But most of all I was impressed by the Masses. I was main celebrant at one English Mass and said Mass in the Apparition Room. I had a distinct sensation of Mary's presence when blessing the religious articles for the people after Mass. I felt at home and at home with everyone I met there.

I truly have not felt the same since. The Mass, the Divine Office, Christ in the Eucharist and in my fellow man, has ever growing meaning. Praise the Lord!

THE FIRST DAYS

Fr. Jozo Zovko, O.F.M.—Medjugorje

The man who didn't believe in those first days is speaking to you. But now I believe—I very much believe. I would like to tell you why I didn't believe and why I believe now. I would like to invite you and tell you why you should accept this and believe.

Six years, three months and twenty-one days ago, Our Lady decided to choose Medjugorje and to get in touch with the Church. We still haven't recovered from what she did. The children who first saw her were nearly lost when they tried to tell people what they saw. Nobody believed them at first. Later on, however, it was a different picture. To the unfaithful people, Heaven was starting to talk through the apparitions and many miracles. The sun was turning into a shining mass that moved toward the crowds as if it would consume them. People were afraid.

Then the people started listening to the children with their hearts. The children didn't say anything special except that they saw Our Lady and she blessed them. And she also gave them instructions on a day-to-day basis. That's how the first six days passed.

During that time, various miracles in nature invited people to come, and many said, "Let's go, let's see the miracles." That kind of curiosity was closing my heart, so I said, "No, that's not Our Lady." But it is interesting that all the school children believed the visionaries. The children were the first to believe. And it is also interesting that nobody was envious of them.

I think back to those days when I didn't believe. At that time I had many reasons for not believing, but now I can sum them up into one: I was too proud.

We cannot come to Medjugorje and say, "I want to pray for grace; I want to show Our Lady that I have my plans to help her, and that they should be approved." Medjugorje is the place where Our Lady invites her children to be obedient, to obey like Jesus.

What does Our Lady want of us? When she came into the Church she said, "Convert." I didn't understand that, even though I thought I did. I thought, like all my parishioners, that Our Lady was finally inviting all who had stopped praying, to start again, that she was inviting drunkards to stop drinking, or those who were destroying family life and Church to stop doing that. The next three evenings I gave three sermons about these things. But nobody converted. Really and truly, nobody. Why? How come that I spoke, and nobody heard?

She came with the message of the meaning of conversion, and she invited us to pray. We prayed for a whole afternoon. Our Lady said that we should pray the Rosary every day. The people seemed happy and joyful, and that day they decided not to go home, but to continue in prayer. They all felt that Our Lady was joyful because of our prayer.

That same day, after the Mass and during the prayer, Our Lady appeared in Church. She blessed the gathered people. She was full of joy. Then I said to the gathering, "You who believed were right! Our Lady is really here." The people were glad my faith was awakened. We prayed all night and gave thanks. The people started spreading Our Lady's message to pray, and they intensified prayer in their own homes.

But our prayer wasn't always the prayer of love. Our Lady brought us a message saying, *Don't pray with your lips; when you pray, pray with your heart.* I had trouble understanding that, and Our Lady spoke to me in my heart, and to the visionaries. She said:

> *Today, before prayer, may every one of you forgive your neighbor. Today may everyone find in his heart all of his enemies, and may he show them to the Father with joy. May he pray for them. Let him wish full joy and blessing upon them.*

I thought it was simple.

In the afternoon I told all the people what Our Lady had said and asked them if they understood me. And all of them said, "Yes." "Can you do that?" I asked. Everyone was silent, and it was an uneasy situation, turning into endless desert. I was a little afraid, and I tried to enter that desert with my voice and said, "We will try now to pray for conversion, for the gift of forgiveness."

There was silence for about twenty minutes. It was terribly long. We didn't know where to go.

Then the greatest miracle in Medjugorje that I know of happened. The church was crowded with people, and one man in the middle of the church shouted with a powerful voice:

"Jesus, I have forgiven!"

And he went on, crying bitterly.

Suddenly, that's what every one of us did. Can you imagine, thousands of people crying, and praying, "Jesus, I have forgiven, forgive me!" Everyone was looking for a hand to squeeze and to say, "Forgive me!" It went on for a long time, and we went on praying Rosaries after that. It was an unforgettable prayer.

Our Lady let us experience something that was absolutely new. We felt that a whole new space of prayer was in our hearts. We felt, as if from an immense well, from deep in our hearts, that prayer was pouring out into the world, giving love, joy and happiness. It was the great prayer.

After that, we celebrated the Mass. It was truly a feast of love. We experienced something mystical, something wonderful, as if we were sitting at supper with Jesus. He was present with us on the altar—everybody felt that. The teachings of Medjugorje had begun. (From a homily, October 15, 1987 in Medjugorje.)

* * *

Fr. Bob Bedard

"I am convinced that Medjugorje is authentic, but I'm not hung up on it. If the competent Church authority rules one day that these apparitions are not worthy of belief, I will submit at once and say so publicly.

"In the meantime, we can hardly go wrong if we follow the basic call the Blessed Mother is reported to be making from her post in a remote valley in Yugoslavia. She urges repentance, turning back to the Lord, plus lots of prayer, fasting and penance, that millions of others will do the same. Authentic or not, Medjugorje has plenty to recommend it." (From *Medjugorje Reflections,* Koinonia Publishers.)

PEACE

Fr. Richard McSorley, S.J.—Center for Peace Studies
Georgetown University, Washington, D.C.

When I was asked by a pilgrimage director to lead a group to Medjugorje, I knew nothing about it. He showed me a videotape and I saw that it was a message of peace from Our Lady given in a Communist country. That seemed enough for me to find it very interesting.

I went four times and visited the visionaries, the priests and the pilgrims. I interviewed them and asked them four questions: 1) Is the main message of the Blessed Mother peace? 2) Did the Blessed Mother's demand that we love everyone include atheists? 3) Does this mean that we should not kill anybody, not even atheists? 4) Could a person who understands the message of Our Lady, in good conscience, conclude it is wrong to prepare to kill because it is wrong to kill?

The answers to the first three questions were clear and immediate. "Yes." The answer to the last question was puzzling to many people. They asked what I meant by that. I explained that since it's wrong to kill, preparing to kill is also wrong and we in the United States are preparing to kill by spending money for weapons of death, by spending so much of our time and training to teach people to kill. Many other countries are doing the same. After it was cleared up what was meant, the general answer, with some variations like, "Well, sometimes there might be an exception," was, "Yes, it is wrong to prepare to kill."

I think that this message, and the prayers and fasting of the millions who visited Medjugorje, affects peace in the world and helped to end the Cold War more than any other influence.

SHE CAME TO ME

Fr. Bernard A. Tonnar, S.J.—New Orleans, Louisiana

In 1986 I heard for the first time about Medjugorje—five years after Our Lady began to appear. My friends offered to send me two books on these events. They came and I opened one to find the name of a nun who was Charismatic. I closed the book, called my friends and said, "This is Charismatic. I want no part of it." I'm not against the Charismatic Movement, but I felt I was not called to it. So Medjugorje faded away until I was moved to my present assignment. There, I heard many speak about it. My one reframe was, "If you want to believe in Medjugorje, fine. But I'm skeptical. If the Blessed Mother wants me to believe, She will let me know. She will come to me."

In 1988 I got a phone call from a lady. She wanted an appointment. I had never seen her before and did not know her name. She wanted to share with me an experience she had.

This is what she told me: "I haven't been inside a Catholic church for eighteen years although I was raised a Catholic. I hated everything about the Church—priests, nuns, whatever. Recently, I heard two of my co-workers speak about Our Lady appearing in a place called Medjugorje. I walked away because they mentioned Mary. But the word Medjugorje would not leave my mind. A few days later I read in the newspaper about a man giving a talk in a Catholic Church about his experience at Medjugorje. I read it several times and asked my husband if he would go with me. He said, 'If you enter that Catholic Church it will collapse.' We went. Halfway through the man's lecture I began to have a warm feeling. My hatred for the Church was leaving me. When I walked out of the church all my hatred was gone. Even my husband noticed the change."

She stopped talking. Finally, I said, "I really appreciate you sharing this with me. It is a spiritual miracle that has been given you." She looked at me and said, "You don't even know my name." "No. What is it?" And then a ton of bricks fell on me. "Miriam."

Miriam! Our Lady's Hebrew name. She had come to me in a very strange way. But she came, and I began to believe in Medjugorje. From that moment my whole life has changed.

95

"ON-SITE INSPECTION" MEDJUGORJE

Fr. Bernhard Philbert, Priest and Physicist

In itself, I had no need to go to Medjugorje. From the many reports that I had heard I was quite convinced that miracles were happening there and that faith was being awakened there. However, because many bishops and archbishops—and also the Marian movement, albeit for opposite reasons—wanted it, I traveled yet once to Medjugorje. And I must say, I thought to myself beforehand that there I would see no miracles in the true sense. But what I really saw was **the Miracle of Confession and of Conversion.** There I heard confessions for hours on end, from early until late at night, and every day, and I have *never* in my entire life experienced this kind of deep conversion by people. Therefore, the fruits of repentance and of penance in Medjugorje are good.

I would not like to consider myself at all competent here, and the question whether it is now ultimately authentic or not, I do not dare to decide either. I see that the fruits are good, are even very good and somehow have even taken on a salvation-historical dimension. So far as I know the messages, the whole thing seems to me to resonate with the proclamation of the Church. From the messages, I see no occasion to be able to make a negative critique. (From *"Medjugorje,"* April, 1991.)

GOD RECLAIMS HIS PEOPLE

Fr. Robert A. Pollauf S.J.—Detroit, Michigan

From October 20 to 27, 1989, I was one of forty-nine pilgrims to Medjugorje sponsored by the Theotokos Apostolate of Toledo, Ohio. Like the Canterbury pilgrims of Chaucer, we were a diverse lot: two priests, three nuns, nine married couples, a divorcee and the rest singles. One Protestant woman came to please her Catholic husband; the divorcee was hoping to put her life together through the intercession of the Virgin Mary; some came out of curiosity; some were skeptical and even at the end of the pilgrimage, a few doubted the authenticity of the visions. For the most part all were driven by varying degrees of faith in God's intervention in His world.

I was impressed by the faith of pilgrims from so many countries as they participated in the Masses, Rosaries, interviews with the visionaries, homilies and talks by the Franciscan Fathers, bus trips, praying together and especially the large numbers going to confession in one of a dozen or more languages. The participation of the pilgrims and the packed attendance at all the Masses was most inspiring. Also, the genuine hospitality of the local people in welcoming us will be long remembered.

Among our pilgrim group there was mutual support and charity as we formed a family. We looked out for one another. An elderly lady of eighty-nine years was literally carried up and down Mr. Krizevac during "The Way of the Cross" by younger men and women in the group.

One incident will always remaid vivid in my memory. It took place on October 25 during the recitation of the Rosary and interview with Maria Pavlovic, one of the visionaries, half-way up "Blue Cross" hill, a site of some of the early appearances of the Virgin Mary. I was hoping to get a picture of Maria. She cooperated as she looked straight at me with a look of vibrant faith and profound peace. I was suffering from a leg ailment and was leaning against a huge rock for support when a feeling of the greatest euphoria, contentment and well-being free of all pain came over me. I felt as if time had stopped and I could remain in this state forever. I was at peace with myself, with the world and with God. It was an experience I shall always remember.

To me Medjugorje means God has not given up on His people. Through Mary we are reminded of the simple basic truths of our faith: prayer, especially communal; fasting (also in a wider sense of self-denial); the Rosary; Holy Mass and the Eucharist; regular Confession; loving one another and overcoming our materialistic tendencies. My own devotion to Mary was greatly enhanced. God still speaks to us through His Blessed Mother.

* * *

I AM GRATEFUL TO GOD FOR MEDJUGORJE

Cardinal F. Tomasek, Primate of Czechoslovakia

Cardinal F. Tomasek, Primate of Czechoslovakia responded in an interview from "Sveta Bastina" in January 1988:

"The events in Medjugorje are important. We have received many graces. Prayer and fasting, faith and conversion, and calls to peace can only come from God alone. I met many pilgrims who went to Medjugorje. They have returned filled with hope and joy in living their faith. I know well some groups of the faithful who have begun to pray and to fast, having learned it in Medjugorje. When the world hinders the announcement of the Gospel, God Himself finds other means to reach His children. I am deeply grateful to God for Medjugorje. Here we are in the 70th anniversary of the apparitions of Fatima in this Marian year, and Medjugorje fits in well within this context. I hear very much talk, but I wish to hear even more about Medjugorje. I will willingly go there as a pilgrim, in order to receive this same hope which a number of my faithful are also seeking there." (From *Eight Years*, The Riehle Foundation.)

FROM AUSTRALIA

Myles McKeon, Bishop Emeritus—Bunbury, Australia

Here is the testimony of Myles McKeon, Bishop Emeritus from Bunbury (Australia), 70 years of age:

"Many people ask me: 'Monsignor, what do you think of Medjugorje?'

"One must wait for the official position before giving an official announcement [...]. But then, each is free to express his personal opinion. Here is mine:

"In Medjugorje I saw the contemplation of priests and laymen. During long hours of prayer, I was one of them. I especially saw hundreds of young people pray the Rosary, on their knees, on the ground. I saw the church of Medjugorje full to the bursting point, crammed, at each Mass. As a priest at Vatican Council II (I was named bishop just a month before the Council), I witnessed many good changes, no sad things. Now we complain that the people have stopped going to confession, that they neglect to pray. In Medjugorje we attend to the restoration of all that. In the evening, at the church, the prayers last three hours and more, and the people stay!

"Everything that takes place in Medjugorje is focused around the Eucharist and that is good. The people return to the Sacrament of Reconciliation, and it is magnificent.

"When one sees all that [...], one can affirm: 'Yes, the Blessed Virgin is present.' One perceives here, in Medjugorje, the presence of Jesus and Mary. Then let us wait [...], while praying, fasting and hoping that the Lord will hear our prayers. God will bless all those who come to Medjugorje and all those who commit themselves in this new grace. I add, may God and Mary be thanked for all that." (Taken from *Eight Years,* The Riehle Foundation.)

A PILGRIM BISHOP FROM IRELAND

Bishop Seamus Hegarty—Raphoe, Ireland

I had heard much about the Medjugorje phenomenon and, as things turned out, managed to go there myself for five days in July 1987. I went, of course as a private pilgrim, a private person.

I couldn't help being enormously impressed by everyone, both local parishioners and those who visit Medjugorje from all over Europe and overseas. I also got a very clear impression that here in Medjugorje you are dealing with a center or prayer, of penance and of reconciliation.

By their fruits you shall know them. Here the fruits are so manifest, so clear and impressive, both in Medjugorje itself and among those who return home after a pilgrimage, that they simply cannot be ignored. Among many people from my own diocese that had been to Medjugorje, I noticed the ongoing, positive results in relation both to their personal and family life. Thus, I felt simply obliged to go to the place and find out for myself the source, the explanation of this experience, this tremendous manifestation of faith, this high and exemplary Christian way of life.

My most outstanding experience in Medjugorje was the hearing of confessions. One day I spent three hours doing so. And I am sure that during those three hours I heard more confessions of the kind that are basic and come from the depths of the heart, than during all the 21 years of my priesthood. I could not help being moved by the workings of grace—the clear workings of grace—also, by the clear acceptance of the call to penance and reconciliation expressed so unmistakably in the quality of confessions I heard. So this experience will ever remain my most impressive and abiding Medjugorje memory. (From *Medjugorje Messenger,* May, 1989.)

INNER HEALING

Fr. Robert DeGrandis, S.S.J.—New Orleans, Louisiana

Medjugorje was a great grace for me since I received a deep inner healing and found prayer very easy during my stay. Although I did not have much religious experience there, I was happy to see the excitement of the people on the pilgrimage.

I have noticed that priests who return from Medjugorje are much more open to religious experience and to the Holy Spirit. They exhibit a greater devotion to Mary also. Many told me that it has been a changing point in their lives. Generally they are much more open to praying for healing with people.

I give priests' retreats around the world, and more and more, priests will admit that they have a new lease on life after Medjugorje. They also have greater boldness in witnessing to other priests on how they have been touched.

Someone has said that there needs to be more freedom among Catholic priests. They have been too rigidly formed and overly intellectual, and Medjugorje frees them up to be themselves, joyful and emotional.

This one fact would be enough to recommend Medjugorje to all priests.

A TIME OF GRACE

Fr. Dale J. Fushek—Mesa, Arizona

The wonderful chain of events started with our trip to Medjugorje. We went there as part of the LIFE TEEN program to tape a television show for teenagers. The experience, personally, was incredible. I have always had a love for Mary, and I've always held her fondly in my heart. But, something changed during our trip. My love for her moved beyond being sentimental, to becoming a relationship with a **person**. The apparitions said to me, loud and clear, that the Blessed Mother is not a plastic statue that we should have respect for. The Madonna, the Lady, is a woman, who shares in the eternal life of her Son, and who God uses to bring the presence of the Son into the world. Mary is real! The apparitions proved to me, and hopefully to all of us, that her unique role in salvation history is still present in the mind of the Father, and that He continues to use her.

The Father is using Mary in my life to deepen my ability to love, and to deepen my commitment to Christ. In the past year, my love for the Mass and for the Eucharist has deepened. My love for the poor has grown. My desire for prayer and to abandon myself is changing. These are gifts that Our Lady is giving to me. She is not "distracting" me from God, from the Son, but she is enlivening my heart with Their love.

God is using Mary for us all. In His mercy, He is sending her into our world to call us to prayer, fasting and conversion. Through her, and through her love, His love is flowing into our hearts. There is no doubt in my mind, in my heart, or in my soul that the apparitions are real! And, there is no doubt in my mind, that God is using Mary for me, for us, to call us to holiness. We must be open to experience this call, and we must listen to the message. It is not her message; she is but a vessel bringing the WORD into the world.

TWENTY REASONS FOR BELIEVING IN MEDJUGORJE

Msgr. Francis Friedl—Dubuque, Iowa

I was invited to go to Medjugorje, but declined for various reasons. The trip was long and tiring; the local Bishop was quoted as saying that the apparitions were a hoax; I myself was skeptical. Then three couples, within 24 hours, approached me with the same request: "Please go to Medjugorje. We would like to make the trip, but we've heard so many contradictory statements about it, that we don't know what to think. If you come back and tell us it is true, we will believe, and we will go." What a load to place on someone's shoulders.

But that is why I went; that is why I kept a journal of the trip; that is why I captioned one page of the journal "Reasons for Believing in Medjugorje," intending to head the opposite page "Reasons for doubting Medjugorje." When I returned, one page was filled, the other was still blank. Let me give you the reasons.

1. *The Taxicabs.* The taxicabs? Well, more specifically the cab drivers. Taxis are the principal means of traveling to the sites in and around Medjugorje. Huge buses bring pilgrims to the five villages surrounding St. James Church through streets so narrow that the vehicles almost touch the houses on both sides. As they pause to deposit their human cargo at various hotels, they block the streets for periods often exceeding 20 minutes, and cabs are forced to wait until the buses can swing around and make their return trip. Can you imagine what the cab drivers in Chicago and New York would do and say when faced with such frustration? But day after day I watched in astonishment as the cab drivers of Medjugorje would open their doors, roll down the windows, light up a cigarette, smile and exchange stories with competing drivers, while waiting for the buses to move. To me, that compares with the miracle of the sun.

2. *The Examinations.* For more than ten years the most experienced and skilled theologians, medical doctors and psychiatrists have examined the seers intensely, and have given no negative reports. One talented child would have difficulty fooling this panel of experts for even a few days; it is not humanly possible for six of them to deceive such an armada of skilled observers for more than ten years.

3. *Father Jozo.* One needs to spend a day with him to understand this reason. He works about 18 hours a day; his homilies and meditations are superb. He himself doubted the apparitions for the first eight days, and is reported to have said that for the rest of his life he would be ashamed of those eight days.

4. *Marinko.* Marinko, uncle of two of the children, together with his wife Dragica, has been as close to the children as anyone. Thousands of times he has been asked the same question: "Did you ever see Mary?" With all the adulation heaped on the children and with the attention of millions focused on Medjugorje, it would be completely understandable if at some point he would say: "Well, yes, perhaps just a brief glimpse." But his answer for the last ten years has always been the same: "No, I never saw her." In some ways, that is a more compelling piece of evidence than the testimony of those who saw Mary.

5. *Maria.* What a charming, delicate, marvelous girl she is. She shuns any applause when she comes to speak and she tries to hide from flashbulbs. Her reason: "Please applaud God only; we have done nothing." Ditto for the other visionaries.

6. *The Children and Money.* Ivan is the only one of the children whose family is well-to-do. The children obey carefully the intruction they say they have received from Mary: they are to accept no money from visitors; even when they share a room in their home with a visitor, they are not to accept payment.

7. *The Shopkeepers.* I have visited bazaars and border city shops all over the world, and am used to being pushed and haggled by shopkeepers, especially at shrines. I found none of that at Medjugorje. If you wish to buy, you are treated with courtesy. If you decline, there is no urging. In fact, nearly every time I bought a few medals or rosaries, the shopkeeper insisted that I accept a nice gift in addition to my purchases.

8. *The Franciscan Shop.* Next to St. James Church the Franciscans operate a shop for purchases of rosaries, medals and holy cards. It is tiny and confined; the doors are closed whenever Mass is being offered at St. James. It would be a simple matter to double the income: enlarge the shop and keep it open at all hours.

9. *The Collections.* After hearing the desperate pleas of American TV evangelists to give generously so that God might spare the

life of the speaker, it was a revelation to see the collections taken up at the Masses in St. James Church. At the offertory a lay assistant passes around wicker baskets; no mention is made of the collection; no pressure is put on the congregation. The expenses of caring for the crowds is considerable, and the collections are necessary. I am told that much of what is not needed for the parish is given to help other needy parishes.

10. *Faith of the Villagers.* Prior to the apparitions, the villagers, while strong in their faith, were quite average in their attendance at Mass and their devotion to the Rosary. Today one sees the Rosary everywhere, even in the hands of women tending sheep in the pastureland leading to St. James Church. The daily Croatian Mass is so crowded it is difficult for travelers to find even standing room in the Church.

11. *Courtesy of the Villagers.* There are hundreds of examples. Let me give just one. I was kneeling on the hard floor in the back of Church one day, having come late for the Croatian Mass. I heard a loud "Psst," looked over and saw a women who must have been well in her 80s, sitting on a fold-up stool she had brought. She waved to me to take the stool. *No way* would I take the chair of an octogenarian and let her kneel on the pavement! But she made such a fuss that I had no choice but to accept her kindness. Another: Marinko giving up his room for a couple who came unexpectedly, saying, "I was always taught to look on anyone who came to my door in need as if it were Jesus."

12. *Courtesy of the Pilgrims.* One sees on every side what was once remarked by a pagan of the early centuries: "See these Christians, how they love one another." The courtesy of visitors is demonstrated in the crowded Masses in St. James Church, but never more powerfully than on the steep inclines of Mt. Krizevac. One of the wonders of Medjugorje is how the lame, the halt and the blind can make that difficult trip over slippery, jagged rocks, often made more treacherous by rains, without serious injury. The answer: the pilgrims help one another at every turn of the path.

13. *The "Hills."* Call them hills if you like, but the Hill of Apparitions and Krizevac are mountains. One of the amazing things is to see people, whose health would have prevented them from walking through the mall in their home towns, climbing both. Many climb barefoot.

14. *The Eucharist.* I have never seen such a longing for the Eucharist as I have seen at Medugorje. Especially is this found in lapsed Catholics. Leading to #15:

15. *Sacrament of Reconciliation.* One of the most notable features of Medjugorje, distinguishing it from other apparition sites, is the number and intensity of confessions. People flock to the sacrament in every language; hundreds of estranged Catholics return to the Church every week.

16. *Reconciliation of the Villagers.* Marinko tells how there used to be a great animosity among the villagers. Cursing one another was common. Then the Church was built. Fr. Jozo preached on reconciliation and asked them to be friends; he paused, said he would not continue until they were reconciled with one another. Finally one old man walked over and put his arms around an enemy. The entire congregation followed suit. The villagers were healed. They still are.

17. *The Music.* One has to hear the beautiful Croatian songs to Mary echoed by thousands of pilgrims each in their own language, to enjoy uplifting liturgy.

18. *Sisters, Priests, Bishops.* They come from all over the world, including now even Yugoslav Bishops, to attend and concelebrate one of the six daily Masses. On their return home, thousands of laity, priests, religious and bishops attend literally hundreds of gatherings in honor of Mary in every country and, without reservation, give public testimony to their belief in Medjugorje.

19. *Through Mary to Jesus.* One of the most convincing evidences of the validity of the apparitions is the fact that while Mary is the principal attraction bringing people to Medjugorje, every message leads away from her to her Son. The result is not an extreme form of adulation of Mary, but an increased commitment to the Mass, the Eucharist and the Sacrament of Reconciliation.

20. *The Signs.* In addition to the claims of rosaries turning color and the "miracle of the sun," there have been many healings attested by doctors. Some of those who have been healed, I know personally. I saw one special sign while at Medjugorje that I would rather not describe; it is sufficient to say that it was one that brought me to my knees, and made me wonder why I had even been so skeptical.

I accompanied a group on a pilgrimage to Medjugorje in October of 1989 with the somewhat bemused air of a priest seeking to satisfy his curiosity about the growing number of reports coming from that little village concerning a series of apparitions which defied all the existing rules of Marian appearances...too long, too many, too simple in message content, too regular in schedule, etc....yet with the conviction that if I am to be a source of spiritual growth for people, I should not remain totally ignorant of a topic so widely discussed and personally experienced by friends on every side.

I returned from Medjugorje with a hunger to find out everything I could about this remarkable series of events.

* * *

ONE OF NUMEROUS VOCATIONS BORN IN MEDJUGORJE

Fr. Dom Matteo—Settignano, Italy

Seven years ago, I went to Medjugorje almost by chance. I was a fourth-year student at the University; I was 23 years old, with the best possibilities of work and integration into the world. But, having returned home, I experienced a very strong desire for a total consecration in the religious life and the priesthood. I left everything. I entered a monastery and, by the grace of God, I have been a priest today for 20 days (October 20, 1990). Two days after my priestly ordination, I returned to Medjugorje through a play of various circumstances, as though the mother wanted me to reinforce the ring which she had opened here, or rather affix her seal on this vocation. My heart overflowed with joy during all the days that I spent there. I cried to her my thanks. To me it seemed almost a dream of being able to be here and to celebrate the Divine Mysteries.

To the young people who listen to the same mysterious call in Medjugorje, I say:

—Do not be afraid to thrust yourselves into it. Do not look at what you are leaving, but what you are gaining, because if you thrust yourselves into it, you will end, completely straight into the arms of Mary, the Most Blessed Virgin, who will never leave you. Our Lady of Medjugorje continues to call. Why not listen to her?

TWO SIBLING PRIESTS GIVE WITNESS

(1.) Father Armand Girard, S.SS.A.

It is difficult for me to draw any conclusions about that pilgrimage to Medjugorje, because that pilgrimage was so full of grace that I feel I've really said nothing. I want to emphasize that my fears were dissipated by the constant presence of the Virgin Mary. This mother that Jesus gave us from the Cross protected me in such an obvious way that in spite of all the things that happened, which could have been maddening or even serious, I never felt the slightest anxiety. Why be afraid? Our Mother is with us. Day after day, she showed me the way, guiding me with the delicate embrace of motherly love. It was probably the first time that my blind eyes were opened to the spiritual dimensions of the divine maternity of Mary.

This pilgrimage helped me to understand that honoring the Blessed Virgin is not an extra devotion that we should have. Her presence in our priestly life is an absolute necessity. Mother of Christ the priest, she is the very air that surrounds all our pastoral activities.

To conclude this testimony, I want to say to those who will read it: The call of the Blessed Virgin is the call of the Gospel:

Pray, Pray often
Go to Confession every month
Fast on bread and water, especially on Fridays
Do Penance
Abandon yourself to the Father's Will

It is in complete submission to the authority of the Church that I wrote this testimony. It was impossible for me not to say what this pilgrimage has meant to me personally.

(2.) Father Guy Girard, S.SS.A.

1. Those ten days in Medjugorje allowed me to meet most of the visionaries. My contact with them convinced me that they are perfectly normal and well balanced.

2. The parishioners are people of prayer with a remarkable, dynamic faith. They challenge us by their lives of prayer, fasting and charity.

3. The priests and nuns are witnesses of God. Their fervent sermons are nourished by prayer. They are not looking for glory but try to answer the needs of the parishioners and pilgrims with a tireless patience.

4. The numerous conversions are already a remarkable sign that the Virgin Mary's call has been heard.

5. What the Blessed Virgin is asking for: Peace, Faith, Daily Prayer (Rosary), Penance (especially fasting), Holy Communion and the Sacrament of Reconciliation, all these are already demanded by the Gospel. The Virgin Mary is putting us back into the heart of Jesus' message.

I am writing this testimony to thank the Blessed Virgin Mary for all she is doing for us. And also to assure the priests, the men and women religious, as well as the parishioners of Medjugorje of my prayers so that they may be faithful witnesses of all that the Blessed Virgin is asking.

(Taken from *Mary, Queen of Peace—Stay With Us,* Editions Paulines.)

* * *

Fr. George Tracy

At Medjugorje, Mary is really fulfilling and completing Fatima. Her message is one of deep urgency. It tells us that the recipe for co-redemption is prayer, the Eucharist, the Rosary, fasting, and that it will take a renewal of the human heart to bring order into the world.

The objectors to Medjugorje don't understand that. I can only speak of it by the results. I spent a hundred hours in the fields there hearing confessions of people, some of whom hadn't been to confession in 30 years. There were 20,000 youths there last week; imagine that. Conversions are taking place all the time, in a peaceful way. There is simply a deep joy there in the presence of Mary, nothing hysterical at all. And people keep coming back. I don't know why the bishops don't approve it. I wish they'd all go and see for themselves. (Excerpted from Gerald M. Costello's article in the September 7, 1989 edition of *Catholic New York*.)

THE SPIRIT OF MEDJUGORJE

Fr. Duaine Cote—Mayville, North Dakota

It was in the fall of 1985 when I first heard about the Blessed Virgin Mary's appearance in Medjugorje, Yugoslavia.

These reported apparitions at Medjugorje have not yet received explicit approval by the Church, but this is not unusual, because the Church always proceeds cautiously in such matters. But when Pope John Paul II was asked if people could go to Medjugorje, he reportedly said: "Ah, Medjugorje! If they pray and do penance when they go there, let them go, let them go." During the past year I learned of many priests who had gone there as spiritual directors to the faithful, on private pilgrimages. Soon I found myself really longing for the opportunity.

Apparently it was the Lord's will that I make this pilgrimage, because I was able to purchase my passport and visa very quickly, and everything else seemed to just fall into place for me to make the trip. We arrived in the village on Sunday, April 10, 1988 at 3:30 p.m. and after getting settled in our homes in the village, there was still time to go to church for the three-hour service that occurs every day from 6:00 to 9:00 p.m.

Literally every inch of space in St. James Church was packed with local village people and pilgrims from all over the world. What a powerful phenomenon this was in itself. I was deeply touched by the atmosphere of faith, peace, prayer and inner conversion of people's lives that I experienced there.

I personally experienced the inner conversion of people's hearts in the Sacrament of Reconciliation, as I heard confessions several hours each day, conversions of people who had been away from the church five, ten, twenty years or more, as well as those who had been going to church but were moved by the grace of God to make a beautiful confession.

Other occasions of special grace for me were the continual prayer pilgrimages on rugged, rocky paths to the top of Apparition Hill and Cross Mountain, located on either side of Medjugorje, the large crowds of people attending Mass in various languages throughout the day, and the continual stream of people in and out of St. James Church to spend time in prayer.

Probably the peak moment of my time there occurred the first day, when I arrived at the cross on Apparition Hill, which marks the spot where Mary first appeared to the visionaries in June 1981. I seemed to sense a special presence of Mary and Jesus at that moment, so I just knelt there in prayer for some time before continuing on my pilgrimage. From my experience at Medjugorje, I feel called to more intense prayer and weekly fasting.

What the visionaries are saying is very simple: "We have seen the Madonna, the Mother of God, the Gospa," (as they say in Croation). Personally, I believe the messages and events occurring there are very authentic, because they coincide so well with the Gospel message. It remains to the Holy Spirit to verify this. (From *The Silver Book,* The Riehle Foundation.)

* * *

Rev. Michael Koonsman

The ecumenical dimension was further highlighted by the presence of Father Michael Koonsman, an Episcopalian (Anglican) priest from the Bowery in the heart of New York City, who said his own life has been incredibly blessed by six (!) visits to Medjugorje. (Reflections of Fr. Bob Bedard).

TIME WITH THE BLESSED SACRAMENT

Fr. Ralph J. Dyer, S.M.—East St. Louis, Illinois

It is difficult to piece together the many remarkable experiences I have had in Medjugorje. I went there as one of two spiritual directors for a group of pilgrims. What seems to predominate in all these experiences are the precious moments I was to spend in the presence of the Blessed Sacrament. The Sacred Host was exposed in a side chapel of one of the new buildings which had been built since my last visit to Medjugorje in September 1989. I was able in my very busy schedule to have some time there. Two prayerful experiences which highlighted my trip:

With Vicka: Gordana, a professional tour-guide and dear friend of the visionaries, brought Fr. Peter Blake and me to Vicka's room. It was the room where Vicka visits frequently with Our Lady. Vicka prayed over both of us. When she laid hands on our heads we both felt a heavy weight of the Holy Spirit. Her hands were like a weighty piece of iron resting on our heads. And when she said goodby, she embraced each of us!

Satan: While the prayerful experience with Vicka proved to me beyond a doubt that Mary is powerfully present in Medjugorje, Satan too, is present. This is not surprising as Our Lady has often asserted that he would be. He is raging—angered because his kingdom is quickly being destroyed.

Miracles continue to recur daily...One of these occurred as our group ascended Krizevac (the Cross Mountain) praying the Stations of the Cross as we climbed. One of our group, a diabetic, who was unable to go twenty feet up the smaller hill, Podbrdo, insisted on climbing the much more difficult mountain of Krizevac. At the fourth station, the excruciating pain in her back suddenly disappeared. She wept profusely and climbed with considerable ease to the very top! The next day when she awakened in the morning, she tested her legs which no longer seemed to have the morning pain she ordinarily experienced and felt herself healed of it, too.

SIN AND CONVERSION

Fr. Philip Pavich, O.F.M.—at Medjugorje

Words! You know, there have been enough words said and ink spilt to save the whole world, the whole universe, many times over. Words won't save the world, that is not the answer. These messages are not words.

The primary way for us to spread this message is that we become a message—that my life, my whole behavior, my whole style of living in Jesus, becomes the primary message. The need for all of us is to incarnate this whole reality of conversion and of turning our hearts over to God.

This morning I had occasion to read the first several weekly messages from Our Lady, and I didn't realize that Our Lady had expressed, what she called "two wishes." In the very first message she said,

Dear Children, I have chosen this parish in a special way and I wish to lead it.

Her first wish: I wish to lead it, protect it, and I want everyone to be mine. Then the next week she said,

Dear children, in this parish, I want you to start converting...in that way all who come here will be able to convert.

This was the second wish, that people would convert because you have converted. If we could really convert, she says, then other people will be touched or moved through you instruments of grace.

She also expressed something very touching, that same month, about the sufferings of Jesus. She said that she wanted us to persevere in trials and difficulties, to just think about and ponder how the Almighty, even today, suffers because of our sins. She said the Almighty, her Son, is still suffering, today, because of our sins.

Those first weeks of those weekly messages, Our Lady spoke some very profound, elementary truths: her wish that she wanted to lead us, and her second wish that we all convert, and that if we do, then others would actually turn to God because of our conversion.

She also stressed the Heart of Jesus and how it is inflicted with all kinds of sin. I wish all of you could have the viewpoint of a priest who hears confessions here. You and I are all individuals. I have my own sin history, you have yours. But, for the many hours that I hear confessions here, I can appreciate the variety of Our Lady's expression. *He is offended by all kinds of sins.* All kinds, all types! Thank God you and I are only one. But I think Our Lady has a view none of us can appreciate. She has this view of "all kinds of sins" that terrible variety of sin that offends the Sacred Heart of Jesus, of her Son.

So she is calling us in a very touching, maternal, compassionate way to this reality.

Do you believe in sin? Do you?

We always ask: Do you believe in Jesus? Do you believe in God the Father Almighty? Yes! Do you believe in Jesus Christ His only Son Our Lord? Yes! Do you believe in the Holy Spirit? Folks, the belief in Jesus Christ, who became man and died for our sins, is explicit, which brings us to this very question:

Do you still believe in the reality of sin?

This is something we all need to face. Sin is a doctrine of our faith. Sin is an element of the Creed. The existence of sin is a revelation of God. God revealed the quality and existence of sin.

One of my amazements here, as a confessor, is that people are blinded to the reality of sin, and how Our Lady touches them here. They somehow get the grace here to all of a sudden believe in sin again. There is this great awakening.

I realize this is not a popular subject for preaching, and it is not "in" today. You are not supposed to talk about sin. You know, we all found fault with the Church: "In the old days all they did was talk about sin." But now we have renewal, and we have joy, and we have song, and we have a merciful, compassionate God, and we have certainly taken the focus off of this reality of sin.

Well, here it pops up again. "Do you believe in sin?"

Believing in the reality of sin is essential and correlative to the concept of Jesus, the name of Jesus. When Mary was given the name of Jesus, the Angel said, *Call him Jesus. His name will be Jesus.* In Hebrew, this name meant "God-Savior," because He will be God saving His people from their SINS. It doesn't say that

He is going to do anything but save His people "from their sins."

So, if we diminish, if we lose the reality of sin, do you realize you thereby diminish or lose faith in Jesus as a Savior? Jesus and sin are linked in this particular sense, in that His very function, His very name, His vocational reality, is to save us from sin. Therefore, the Church never allows us to get away from the reality of Jesus and this linkage and reality of sin.

The very first recorded words of Jesus' ministry were on the shore of Galilee, where Jesus lived for three years, where He began to announce His theme. It is recorded in *Matt.* 4:12-17:

Jesus went down to Capernaum, by the sea, to fulfill what had been said through Isaiah the prophet, to heathen Galilee...From that time on Jesus began to proclaim this theme: 'Reform your lives!' The kingdom of heaven is at hand.

He was saying: Convert! Turn back to God! So He expresses in His very first words in public, *Reform your lives.* That is, give up sin; I have come to take it away. He was pointed out by John as the one:

Who takes away the sin of the world, the Lamb of God!

John preached repentance and the conversion of sin, a baptism for the remission of sin. John's function as a fore-runner of Jesus, was to Baptize for the repentance of sin, to prepare a people eager to receive, a people who would have clear vision to recognize Jesus when He came. So, when John would say, "Look, there He is! There is the Lamb of God; there is He who takes away the sin of the world; go to Him," they would see Jesus.

There is something happening today, among us, that is very dangerous to the concept of Jesus as a Savior, and I see this as an evil deception among so many, because we are simply creatures of our day.

Let me put it in a personal context. In the sixties, after Vatican II, I started additional studies at Loyola University in Chicago, in a priest counseling course, a client-centered counseling course. It was the "in thing." From it, I learned that the best thing a priest could do was to have what I call a "go-fer" ministry—a ministry that would mean knowing where to send people to "go for" help. A supposedly smart priest knew that he couldn't really do anything, but he knew where to go for help. He knew all the resources of the community who could "really" help people. I felt myself getting more and more torn down as a priest.

Part of the emphasis was that in client-centered work, you don't tell people what to do. We were getting the message that "you guys have been deformed in your old theology. You priests have just been dictating, telling people what to do, and you don't have compassion, and you don't understand, etc." The correct concept was that man or woman, left to himself or herself, would always make the right choice; so don't impose your values on people. Folks, I was learning this in the early sixties. That's part of the bad fruit we have inherited.

This has spread through the whole Church now. Don't impose your values on people. Just leave them alone. Just pick up the feeling, and reflect back to them, and they will make their own correct choice. I remember our professor there had to face his own crisis when one of his clients committed suicide, when the patient didn't make this alleged self-correcting, right choice.

It was implicit in this new doctrine "of the goodness of man," that we have a natural inherent goodness by which we always choose the correct, the right thing. Gee, my initial Church teaching had always said that man is tilted, because of Original Sin, and that if it is a battle between me and Satan, I'll lose, because he is smarter than I am, he's more clever than I am and so seductive, that I can't take him on, one-on-one. I'll lose every time. My conscience isn't enough. I need a Savior, I need someone to team up with to save me from sin.

So, if you take this new doctrine and run it out to its consequences, one of the fruits that it bears—that infected convents and priests and infected the entire Church—is that we had all been reduced to "go-fers." And if you didn't have the hyphenated priest-hood (if you weren't a priest-dash-psychologist, priest-dash-psychiatrist, priest-dash-social worker, or priest-dash-something) you really didn't have much to offer anybody. Just being a priest of Jesus Christ and ministering really wasn't quite enough. I myself, by 1969, had my own full-fledged vocational crisis and was ready to sign my name on the dotted line with thousands and thousands of other priests, who were quitting the priesthood.

As I look back, I see now what happened. It is a deformation or bad fruit that has affected us today—a falsehood that you can make up your own mind. No one can tell you what to do. So priests don't even try to form anybody's conscience anymore. That's taboo! Now-a-days, some priests just say that if you really think it is OK for you, if you think birth control, etc., is OK, then it is not a sin for you.

Folks, that is pure poppycock. That is simply not true. No one is entitled to delude themselves in making their own little ivory tower conscience, unaffected by Jesus Christ, and unaffected by His Church and by its teaching authority. If you take that client-centered counseling doctrine, and take it to its logical consequences, then nobody has the right to tell you anything. All they have to do is "be compassionate." If I am compassionate with you, you will make the right choice every time.

Well, then what did we need Jesus for? Why did He even bother to come and save us from sin, if there isn't any?

This blown out of proportion compassion means that you can do just about anything, just as long as you have compassion. And compassion then becomes a primary value of lifestyles now. It is in the Church today. Compassion is at the top of the list, and because of compassion, you can sleep around, do drugs, get divorced, annulments, homosexuality, go to the Sacraments, regardless, it's OK, it's between Jesus and you. Follow your conscience. Nobody can interfere with your conscience.

Folks, that is a fabrication, and a destruction of Jesus Christ. That nullifies a Light that came into the world to heathen Galilee. That's like saying leave heathen Galilee alone, just be compassionate, and it will find its own way.

Jesus came to heathen Galilee and started to proclaim this theme: *Reform your lives.* Don't just stick with your own privatized conscience. Reform your lives. He came to tell us what is sin, and what isn't.

There is an objective basis of reality for forming our conscience, and *no* priest has the right to tell you to do what you want, that it's OK. That kind of high priority value of compassion, can enable anyone to receive the Eucharist, sin or no sin. It says you can't tell people what's wrong in their lives. If that doctrine is true, then how can anybody ever convert? How could Jesus have the nerve to come and say, *Reform your lives?* How dare He come and try to tell me what I should change in my life?

Jesus came to save His people from their sins, and I say, "Alleluia!" And I say to you, while you are here in Medjugorje, seek your chance to make a Sacramental Confession. Come with contrite hearts and ask the Lord to show you,

> "Where am I being deluded? What have I been doing
> in my life that really is not in conformity with the Light
> of Christ?"

Let Jesus back into the dark spaces of your life. He wants to be the Light, to a Church, a world, a people, that is very much in need of His light. That light will shine in your heart, if we really seek Jesus and His way.

His Mother echoes His words, when she said, *My first wish is to be with you and lead you...you belong to me and my Son.* Her second wish is that you be converted. That is really fundamental doctrine of who Jesus Christ is, and she is His Mother. She *knows* who He is. She is calling us also to this Sacramental Confession. It is a big call for some, big changes of lifestyles for some. It is conversion.

I say all this not in any sense of wanting to condemn anybody, for I'm part of the system. It's simply a request to get our act together, examine our consciences against the teaching of Jesus Christ and His Church, not against our own isolated, privatized, consciences. May the Lord come into that, and may He shed His light into whatever in you is heathen Galilee, because He came to be that Light of the world.

THE MESSAGE OF MARIAN APPARITIONS

Fr. Peter Toscani, O.S.A.—Philadelphia, Pennsylvania

Apparitions indicate the constant and urgent message for mankind's conversion and peace. Lourdes and Fatima have the Church's approval; Garabandal and Medjugorje have not received official approbation. Since these revelations contain prophetic elements, the Church waits for their possible fulfillment before passing judgment on them; for example, thirteen years elapsed before the approval of Fatima even though 70,000 people witnessed the miracle of the sun. Nonetheless, the Church grants us an option to believe in non-approved apparitions, provided that they contain nothing contrary to Catholic faith or morals.

It is important to maintain the distinction between the authenticity of the apparitions and the teaching of their messages. While the local bishops of Garabandal and of Medjugorje have expressed denial of the supernatural origin of the alleged apparitions in their respective dioceses, they have affirmed the soundness of the messages. This was expressly stated in 1963, by Bishop Eugenio Beitia, of Garabandal; and likewise by Bishop Zanic, who after voicing objections to the divine nature of events at Medjugorje, asserted the validity of the messages.

However, the question of why Mary comes to Medjugorje deserves a direct answer. From the messages from Mary to the six youngsters receiving the visions, we understand that Mary comes as catechist, a teacher, to restate the basic truths of our religion and to clear up the confusion in religious education. She comes as Scripture exegete to demythologize the demythologizers. She comes as Eucharistic promoter to repair the harm and neglect of Jesus in the Blessed Sacrament.

The seers have said that the highlight of their day is not the apparition, but the daily Mass. In fact, the center of Medjugorje for the pilgrims is the evening Mass. Mary comes to Medjugorje especially as our weeping and sorrowful mother, pleading for a return of all children to her Divine Son. She is the Immaculate and Sorrowful Mother—the first title was freely given to her by God, the second she received "the old-fashioned way, she earned it," at the foot of the Cross where, by her compassion, she shared in the Passion of Christ for our redemption.

Mary comes to win sinners back to God. She begs them to accept her message of peace by means of faith, prayer, fasting, reconciliation and conversion. The visionaries have been asked by Our Lady to announce this message to the villagers, the pilgrims and the world. The people have responded to these requests in remarkable numbers these past years: thousands present for daily Mass; millions have gone to confession here; tens of thousands have acquired the practice of Friday fasting on just bread and water; millions are daily reciting the Rosary because of Medjugorje; innumerable conversions have taken place.

In the meantime, we may prudently follow the advice of Lucy of Fatima, Conchita of Garabandal, and the six youths of Medjugorje, who all in effect, state that it is of no use to believe in the apparitions if we do not observe the message. But, it is urgent that we follow the message even if we do not believe in the apparitions. While we may reasonably question or deny credence in apparitions, it would seem rash to ignore their messages, particularly that of Fatima, for as Pope Pius XII wrote: "The time of doubting Fatima is passed," and as Pope John Paul II said: "Fatima is more urgent and more relevant now than ever before."

MEDJUGORJE: A RETREAT

Fr. Robert Faricy, S.J.

I have spent many weeks in Medjugorje. Such gifts! Such grace! The presence of the Holy Spirit! It stays with you: all the memories of the place. Almost always you can find pilgrims around the grounds of the parish church of Saint James and the parish house. Often, especially during the late spring, summer, and early fall, great crowds assemble.

The church, quite large for a parish church, nevertheless often cannot hold all the people who come for the evening Rosary and the Mass. They spill over outside the church.

People come in such large numbers because they believe that the mother of Jesus has specially chosen that place and that parish and that church, that she has visited it in a special way, and that her special presence continues there. And where Mary is, in a special way, so is Jesus. So people come, looking for God, looking for the Lord.

Sometimes the crowding at Medjugorje can become intense. And yet, with all the crowds and the crowding, perhaps partly because of that and partly because all have come for the same purposes, you can find at Medjugorje a wonderful spirit of helpfulness, of cooperation, of love, among the milling crowds of foreigners, Croatians, and villagers, and in the homes where most pilgrims stay. You do not know everyone. You may know no one. But you do know that you are together with everyone in the Lord.

The healings that take place at Medjugorje are signs of the presence of the power of God. They increase our faith. And they show the quality of the Lord's Love.

The Blessed Virgin Mary at Medjugorje has frequently called us to greater faith. She prays for greater faith for each of us, and I can pray with her to Jesus, "Lord, increase my faith!"

What is faith? Faith means not only believing the truths that God has revealed. It includes that, but faith goes beyond agreeing to the truth of Christianity. Faith means believing in Jesus Christ. And in Him is contained all truth; He is the Truth as well as the Way and the Life.

Faith means accepting Jesus' personal call to a close union

with Him, to discipleship, to friendship, to follow Him wholeheartedly. And faith is a gift.

Our Lady at the beginning of her daily visits to Medjugorje identified herself as the Queen of Peace. She applies that title to herself now, in our times, when there is so little peace in the world. And she calls us to pray for peace: peace in the world, among peoples and nations; peace within nations among opposed parties and factions; peace in our own cities and towns and regions, peace in our families; and peace in our hearts.

Medjugorje is truly a retreat. We all need to make it. All of us. As a retreat, it's a conversion that we need to live every day, the rest of our lives. You don't have to go there to do it. He, and His Mother, will come to wherever you are. (From *The Silver Book,* The Riehle Foundation).

WHAT MEDJUGORJE MEANS TO ME

Fr. Kenneth Brockel—Perry, Missouri

I made my first of four trips to Medjugorje three years ago, in 1989. At the time I had been a priest for twenty years. I must admit that I was skeptical about the validity of the happenings in Medjugorje. However, I have been shown the error of my ways, so to speak, by the many blessings I have received and the gifts I have been given during or following each of my four trips.

As a result of my first trip I have "come back to prayer" which I had allowed to falter over the years of my priesthood. I rediscovered the Office, the Breviary, the Rosary.

While on my second trip I prayed that Mary would help me to consecrate my vow of celibacy to the Church. I asked her to "Make it pure as you are pure." Our Lady responded and gave me peace to rejoice in the beauty and joy of celibacy.

During my third trip, a retreat, I was "Slain in the Spirit." The joy and the gifts that were given to Fr. Jozo were given to me. I literally felt the experience of being slain with the Spirit of Jesus and the Spirit of Mary. It was an experience I will always remember.

The blessings I received on the fourth trip were revealed to me on the return trip home. I met a person who had been with Fr. Jozo for a full year. This woman was given the gift of knowing, talking and praying with each person's Guardian Angel. She proceeded to tell me about my Guardian Angel, Jeremiah, who enclosed me with a cocoon and has always protected me. She also told me that I had an archangel, Attende Dominum, (One Who Stands Before the Throne of God). I have always had a great love for my guardian angel and so I was so happy to realize that Jeremiah holds up the Eucharist and Attende Dominum leads a choir of angels in adoration. I was then told by her that in the very near future I would be given a special gift—to wait and pray for this gift. This I am doing. I am certain that Our Lady will help me and bless me with this gift.

I share these joys of Medjugorje because I am firmly convinced that we priests have to be servants of the Lord, just as Mary was. She calls us to a life of service, prayer, and love. I have experienced a re-birth and now I am at complete peace with myself. I now understand our Bishop and I am beginning to walk the way of obedience that Mary calls us to—to follow the Lord Jesus, her Son.

My life has changed since I made that first trip to Medjugorje. It has been enriched by prayer and the fact that I currently belong to two very fulfilling prayer groups. And I am beginning to understand those words of St. Paul which say "May I never boast in anything but the cross of our Lord Jesus Christ, in whom is life and salvation." I pray that all people will understand the beauty and reality of these words.

A REPORT BY A PILGRIM

Fr. José Luis Meza (translated by José Perez)

Since the start of the apparitions of the Virgin on June 24, 1981, the once small village of Medjugorje has quickly become a modern town. The major part of the new construction consists of hotels to house the pilgrims. The rest is small commercial shops and restaurants which serve the public. The area is served by a deep faith. This is an undeniable truth.

Medjugorje is well identified by the towers of the parish church, which has been named St. James. The church, big and strong, is a simple structure and was constructed in recent times. It has been more than a decade since the church seemed so large in relation to the followers who used it. Today, after changes in the hearts of the faithful, it is insufficient in size. Surely this is a verification of a miracle of conversions in massive proportions. Proof of this is evident in the enormous quantity of followers in Medjugorje seeking the Sacrament of Reconciliation. If we compare Medjugorje to other locations well known as sites of pilgrimage, we can say that it is similar to Lourdes, France; Fatima, Portugal; Assisi, Italy; and Guadalupe, Mexico, just to name a few. There is growth in Medjugorje, day by day, because the message of peace that is present is irresistible. The whole world knows what it needs, and in Medjugorje it is being restored.

When the pilgrims pray, the rosary beads adorn their hands; in their words, the faithful are asking for peace in their families, peace for all nations and blessings for all the world. "Peace" ("Mir") is the individual and collective request that is heard in Medjugorje while crossing the streets, singing in the church or visiting the locations of the apparitions in the village of Cernica and Mt. Krizevac. It can be affirmed that Medjugorje is a community of prayer.

Could all this be a simple, collective, contagious psychological phenomenon, or could it be an ecclesiastic truth which demonstrates a real intercessory presence of the Mother of Christ? Nobody doubts that there could be radical attitudes in favor or against the apparitions. But what is quite evident and permits confirmation that something miraculous has happened is that the messages of Mary were not received as propaganda for her own sake. Instead, they proclaim that Christ is the Savior of the world and toward Him we should return to a different type of life, with His intervention.

After a lovely reception given by a generous host family, our small group settled in, attended to by various members of our host family. We learned very quickly about this family's profound faith and the extraordinary kindness exhibited by each member. Any hour we would arrive at the house, they would attend to us in the same fashion of exquisite simplicity and caring. The two youths who prepared our meals caused me to recall the friends of Jesus, Martha and Mary in Bethany.

All the Masses in Medjugorje have a spiritual climate that turns off the tensions of the human heart. They give one a sensation of being under a shade that fortifies a body after having traveled tiringly over a desert. That was the introduction to my spiritual retreat; it was an experience of internal tranquility. One time, after the conclusion of the Eucharistic Celebration, I stayed in the church with the idea to meditate and pray. Personally, during my retreat, I can firmly state that the former model of my life has faded; the retreat collected a definite form: love and belief in God in a way that my ministry is refreshed in the area of evangelism and is effective with the help of the Holy Spirit. I recognize my past weaknesses. I conversed with Mary, a true friend, and from her I received a special blessing. In the nine hours I spent there in the church before her image, I felt neither boredom nor tiredness nor hunger.

In our pilgrimage group there was a single intent and the same interest. Each and every one expressed their hearts. We did not realize that the personal and group level dynamics functioned perfectly in the Christian fraternity. When someone needed help, it was given immediately. When we climbed Mt. Krizevac, praying the Stations of the Cross, it never failed that someone would offer water or a piece of candy. Practically each individual was a guardian angel by my side. Like the disciples of Emmaus, who discovered Christ in the appearance of a stranger (*Luke* 24:13-34), as members of a pilgrim group, we were able to sense the presence of Jesus during misfortunes through the attention and services given us. It was no one's intent to organize us as a social group, but all of us were able to experience the spiritual companionship that happens when people direct themselves to a place God has chosen.

Our group was fortunate enough to see, hear and sense Vicka Ivankovic twice. For one minute I was at her side, feeling an emotion I have experienced very few times—an internal emotion that I felt when I greeted Pope Paul VI for the first time and when I was at the birthplace of Jesus. She squeezed my hands and made supplication for me. I was filled with joy. Without even knowing it, I was saying in a loud voice, "Thank You, Lord, thank You!" My teardrops were hitting the floor. Vicka has not made herself famous by her prophecies and cures, but by her simpleness and humility which are transparent. In her there is no human vanity, and nobody doubts that she has a spiritual energy rarely seen. All her external expressions, manner of speaking, smile, greetings, laughter, etc. sincerely testify to a higher spiritual valor that is an evangelization.

Arriving at Mt. Podbrdo, I paused to meditate near a great rock near the cross. I watched the pilgrims pray, leave their offerings, light candles, touch their rosaries to the cross and meditate in silence. This place has a special similarity to Mt. Tabor. I felt a tranquility so special that I wanted to say, like those friends of Christ, *Lord, how good for us to be here. (Matt.* 17:4). While I was meditating, an Italian lady came beside me and offered me a bunch of grapes. After a long conversation, I asked her to pray for me. She promised to do so and then asked for a blessing. As she left, she gave me a finger rosary (a small metal ring with ten circular beads). I am now using it every day. The gift was given with so much caring and faith. Various times she hugged me. Can it be that the Mother of God makes small apparitions within all women that serve in Medjugorje? One thing was evident—that woman who gave me the grapes and the prayer ring had an apostolic soul that I can never forget.

Visiting priests assist in the ministry of Sacramental Confession. I hung a sign saying, "Spanish speaking," but fortunately my understanding of a few other languages helped me in my pastoral work with those who spoke Italian and English, and even some from Brazil. In Medjugorje, thousands of people go to confession every day. Catholics who had abandoned the Sacrament of Reconciliation for years and years, in Medjugorje, return with special humility and faith. There is no doubt. The miracle is conversion. There can be 20 to 30 priests hearing confessions, and they can never exhaust the lines, especially in the afternoons. Owing to the ministry of Reconciliation, people come closer to the Lord in all the Eucharistic Celebrations.

Everyone who has gone to Medjugorje has their own stories to tell. In telling my story I do not intend to assure or deny anything happening in Medjugorje in regard to the apparitions. What I can affirm and confirm is that all that is written here is the truth.

FRIENDS OF MEDJUGORJE

Fr. Milan Mikulich, O.F.M., S.T.D.—Portland, Oregon

Permit me to introduce myself. I am Father Milan Mikulich, a Croatian Franciscan, however, I do not belong to any Franciscan parish or province of Herzegovina where Medjugorje is located. There are five Franciscan provinces in Croatia. In November 1981, I went from Portland to Medjugorje. I heard Vicka Ivankovic telling me about the apparitions in Medjugorje. From Medjugorje I went directly to Mostar to see Bishop Zanic in whose diocese Medjugorje is situated. "Bishop, what's happening in Medjugorje?" I asked him. Bishop Zanic said, "I am convinced the events in Medjugorje are supernatural and I am also convinced the boys and the girls are sincere and honest and they do not lie. I will defend them in any place." This categorical statement of Bishop Zanic convinced me about the true nature of Medjugorje events. For this reason I began to acquaint the Catholics in America of these apparitions, particularly in my review called *Orthodoxy of the Catholic Doctrine.*

Since 1981 I visited Medjugorje every year and every year I interviewed, with their permission, all the seers separately or all together. I also visited Bishop Zanic every year and with his permission I interviewed him. It is to be stressed that the seers have never contradicted themselves. They always presented the facts as they happened. But Bishop Zanic contradicted himself changing his stand on Medjugorje. In 1986, Bishop Zanic's diocesan commission, selected by him, gave a negative decision and Bishop Zanic told me in his own office that he was going to Rome to declare Medjugorje as a fraud. My response was, "Bishop, I think you are fighting against Our Lady and not against the seers or the Franciscans in Medjugorje." After Bishop Zanic returned from Rome to Mostar, I stopped in Rome on my way back to Portland, Oregon. There I found out that Cardinal Ratzinger told Bishop Zanic to leave his commission's papers and go home. The result of his visit to Rome was not his declaration of fraud in Medjugorje, but a decision of the Holy See to appoint a new Yugoslavian's Bishop's conference to study the Medjugorje events. We must wait for the final decision of the Holy See.

As an epilogue, I would like to mention that Mirjana Dragi-cevic, one of the Medjugorje seers, invited me to perform her wedding to Marco Soldo in Medjugorje on September 16, 1989. On that occasion I extended to them the invitation of a honeymoon in Portland. They accepted the invitation, but for a later date. Since Mirjana had received all of her 10 secrets by Christmas 1982, Our Lady visits her only on her birthday, March 18th, and some other occasions. For the last three years, Our Lady also visits Mirjana on the 2nd day of every month and through her promotes prayer for those of our brothers and sisters who do not believe in God. Keeping in mind the 2nd day of the month, I did everything to have Mirjana come to Portland on the 2nd day of February 1990. When she and her husband Marco arrived, Mirjana said that Our Lady had told her on the 2nd day of January, 1990, that this apparition will take place in our Chapel of Our Lady of Sinj because Bishop Zanic forbids the apparition in a parish church. Thus Our Lady appeared to Mirjana in the Chapel of Our Lady of Sinj.

Mirjana recorded Our Lady's message which was intended for the world. This message has been framed and is placed on a wall in the Chapel of Our Lady of Sinj. In describing Our Lady during the apparition in Portland, Mirjana stated that she appeared very sad because of all those who do not believe in God.

Other books published by...

The Riehle Foundation:

Queen of Peace in Medjugorje
By Jacov Marin
The seven year journal account of a Croatian, diocesan priest on the events of Medjugorje. 224 pages. Color photos.

Suggested donation: $6.50

Messages & Teachings of Mary at Medjugorje
By Fr. René Laurentin
A summary of all the messages and teachings of Medjugorje applied to Catholic doctrine and Scripture. 350 pages.

Suggested donation: $7.00

✝   ✝   ✝

By Fr. Albert Joseph Mary Shamon

Our Lady Teaches About Sacramentals and Blessed Objects
76 pages..$1

Our Lady Teaches About Prayer at Medjugorje
56 pages..$1

Our Lady Says: Let Holy Mass Be Your Life
55 pages..$1

Our Lady Says: Pray the Creed
68 pages..$1

Our Lady Says: Monthly Confession—Remedy for the West
70 pages..$1

Our Lady Says: Love People
70 pages..$2

The Power of the Rosary
44 pages..$2

Apocalypse—The Book for Our Time
94 pages..$4